THE HIGH QUALITY MANAGER

Also by Alfred Tack

MARKETING AND MANAGEMENT BOOKS

Executive Development
Building, Training, and Motivating a Sales Force
How to Overcome Nervous Tension and Speak Well in
    Public
How to Double Your Income in Selling
1000 Ways to Increase your Sales
Sell Better – Live Better
Sell Your Way to Success
How to Train Yourself to Succeed in Selling
How to Increase Sales by Telephone
Profitable Letter Writing
How to Increase Your Sales to Industry
How to Succeed in Selling
How to Sell Successfully Overseas
Professional Salesmanship
Successful Sales Management
Marketing, The Sales Manager's Role
How to Succeed as a Sales Manager
Motivational Leadership

FICTION

The Great Hijack
The Spy Who wasn't Exchanged
The Top Steal
Forecast–Murder
Murder Takes Over
P A to Murder
Death Kicks a Pebble
Selling's Murder
Interviewing's Killing
The Prospect's Dead
The Test Match Murder
A Murder is Staged
Killing Business
Death Takes a Dive
Return of the Assassin

The High Quality Manager

Alfred Tack

Gower

Published by
Gower Publishing Company Limited,
Gower House,
Croft Road,
Aldershot,
Hants GU11 3HR,
England

Gower Publishing Company,
Old Post Road,
Brookfield,
Vermont 05036,
USA

British Library Cataloguing in Publication Data
Tack, Alfred
 The high quality manager.
 1. Management
 I. Title
 658.4   HD31

Library of Congress Cataloging in Publication Data
Tack, Alfred.
 The high quality manager.

 1. Executive ability. 2. Management. I. Title.
HD38.2.T33 1986   658.4'09   85-8105

ISBN 0-566-02606-6

Typeset in Great Britain
by Graphic Studios (Southern) Ltd, Godalming, Surrey.
Printed and bound in Great Britain
by Billing & Sons Limited, Worcester.

Contents

1 The Board meeting

"We need a miracle," said Donald Linklater, "but a miracle forecast is not acceptable collateral for bankers." The Linklater Printing Company, founded in 1882 by Samuel Linklater, had had a member of the family on the Board since that time.

In 1976 the elderly chairman, Donald Linklater, succumbed to the influence of his thirty-year-old nephew, Lionel, and the company entered the field of office appliances. Lionel, seeking new outlets, was sure he had found a winner when he met Swedish engineer, Henrik Lundt, patentee of revolutionary devices for improving the performance of office copiers.

The Lundt copier incorporated the best features of competitive makes, plus a computerised remote control unit enabling documents, drawings, photographs, etc., to be fed into units placed at strategic points throughout a building. The control could be programmed to instruct the copier to select the paper required, photograph the correct number of copies, then collate and store. Even if several instructions were fed into two or three remote controls simultaneously, the main copier could be keyed to accept them in order of priority. The copies were also produced with unmatched speed, clarity and finish, plus full colour – and all in a comparatively small unit.

To the Board Lionel had painted a glowing picture of the future with the new range of copiers, while emphasising the problems associated with the printing industry.

Eventually he dragged the directors still wishing to cling to the past into a great new future of copiers, and then computers.

The investment was high, but the company's conservative policy had enabled substantial cash reserves to be built up. A factory was acquired on the outskirts of Southampton, enlarged, modernised, and equipped with advanced, automated machines.

In those early days Lundt's experience in the copier industry proved invaluable, and two years later the copiers were launched, backed by heavy advertising. The results justified the most optimistic expectations. Sales boomed. Lionel was congratulated, and told repeatedly that Linklaters were fortunate to have such a brilliant young tycoon. But many snags had still to be overcome, and three years on Linklaters had used up all their liquid resources, and the manufacturing time lag and the investment forecast had proved to be hopelessly wrong. Financial assistance had to be negotiated with bankers – only too willing to back Linklaters.

Then the copiers hit serious problems. Breakdowns occurred almost weekly, mostly caused by the computers. Lundt worked hard and produced solution after solution, but all proved to be of a temporary nature. The service division could not cope with the number of calls received. The Board was faced with a critical decision: cut down production until the problems had been solved, increase borrowings, or raise cash by selling the hundred-year-old printing company.

The final decision was to sell, and there were eager buyers, but setback followed setback, and one year later there was again need to go to the banks. But as the months passed, even their massive assistance was insufficient to meet the needs of the troubled company. Everyone, including astute bankers, believed that success was still round the corner. New machinery, an enlarged R&D department, and a factory extension to allow bought out parts to be manufactured under one roof, would solve the cash flow problem in time. They did not! It was then that Linklater approached merchant bankers Scott & Ballinger.

After an investigation, and in co-operation with Linklaters' bankers, a consortium was formed to provide the necessary cash to tide them over. Scott & Ballinger insisted that their own nominee, Richard Hemmings, should be appointed financial director of Linklaters.

After eighteen months of continuing losses in spite of the cost-cutting exercise, Hemmings announced to the Board that the firm was heading for bankruptcy. The banks would no longer give support, and Linklaters' only chance to keep afloat and protect jobs was to find a buyer for the business. The alternative was liquidation. Hemmings, through his friends the merchant bankers, had found such a buyer.

A meeting in the boardroom had been called to enable Hemmings to spell out the details. Round the Chippendale style mahogany table sat the chairman, eighty-year-old Donald Linklater, pink-faced, grey-haired, and slim. Nearly sixty years earlier, a dedicated officer in the Scots Guards, he had answered the family call on the death of his father, resigned his commission, and joined Linklaters. Alongside him, to his right, sat production director Harold Denton. An old servant of the printing company, he had been given the title and directorship for his past services and his loyalty.

In the printing works he had been in his element, but he never matched up to the demands of the office appliance division. Sitting next to him was export director John Ogilvie, a cousin of Lionel Linklater.

On Donald Linklater's left was financial director Richard Hemmings, pale and tight-lipped. He knew he was in for a buffeting. Next to Hemmings sat Jonathan Burley, director of planning. Jonathan was Donald Linklater's son-in-law, a qualified barrister who had given up law to join the family business. Opposite him sat Henrik Lundt, director in charge of research and development, and at the end of the table, facing Donald, was Lionel Linklater.

The chairman opened the meeting with, "This is a sad day in the history of our company. My forebears must be restless in their graves at the plight we are in. We must, however, refrain from apportioning blame. It was a unanimous decision to move away from print and into office appliances and computers. Possibly Lionel's enthusiasm was so contagious that we tended to overlook the problems ahead. Henrik, although so experienced, could not have foreseen the problems which arose and which we have not been able to solve. Without the recession we could, perhaps, have survived. Now that is impossible unless a good fairy provides us with an injection of cash – and there are no good fairies in the banking world willing to loan money without collateral.

"It seems that our only option is to agree to a takeover at a bargain price, if we are to save our employees from unemployment. Yes, it is very sad, but facts have to be faced. Your comments, please."

Lundt, the fair-haired Swede, whose pale face was showing the strain he had been undergoing, said in faultless English, "I am to blame. I should have insisted on more stringent tests, but I am confident that I have now solved all the problems. Can we not find new bankers in Europe or the USA willing to back us?"

"Henrik," said Donald Linklater, "We have approached many financial houses, both here and over-seas. There is, now, no one who would loan us any money. Remember, Henrik, I am of an age when I should be able to retire on my assets, and I find that my most valuable asset is now almost worthless. Thank goodness I have investments in other directions to see me through – so shed no tears for me!"

"I'm sorry," said Lundt.

"May I say something?" asked Lionel Linklater.

Donald shrugged his shoulders and murmured, "We're all here so that each director can express his views."

"Very well," said Lionel, "then I accuse Richard Hemmings of acting against our company's interests. He was, it is true, forced on us by Scott & Ballinger, but we all accepted him in the belief that he was acting in the best interests of the company. It was his duty to put our financial affairs in order. Instead, very quickly, he began negotiating with this Bob Brennan fellow, who is willing to buy us out at a ridiculous price. I persuaded the Board to get out of print and into a growth industry. We made the decision to tackle the office appliance market, and that decision, I believed, was the right one then – and I still believe it is right. What none of us realised was the amount of capital needed to see us through the teething stages."

Hemmings sat back in his chair, fully relaxed. He had listened to so many similar statements in the past, from executives who would never admit that they had been wrong. It was always "unfortunate events which had occurred" or "the recession" or "competition" or a "militant work force" – never the managers' bad judgement. Lionel was no exception.

Hemmings continued to listen, knowing that Donald Linklater had already made up his mind about the future of the company. Lionel went on, "I believe Scott & Ballinger planned to take us over from the very first. They insisted that we employed Richard Hemmings, and now up comes Bob Brennan, also sponsored by the bankers. Who, in the long run, will benefit from this? Why, the bankers, of course! If this Brennan fellow believes we can be successful, then surely we don't need him; what we need is a bank that has faith in us. We should fight on. I repeat, we should fight on!" Lionel, slight, fair-haired, with a wisp of a moustache, gave a good imitation of a Churchillian scowl of defiance.

Donald Linklater said quietly, "I understand your feelings, Lionel, but don't forget, when Richard advised us that our financial affairs were going from bad to worse, we asked him, in the first place, to try to find someone other than the bankers who could bale us out. It was only after he had scoured the market both here and overseas, that the bank finally suggested Mr Brennan. I can't read Brennan's mind – I can't pretend to understand how he intends to turn Linklater's fortunes around but he has had a highly successful past, and has accumulated considerable wealth. Maybe he will make cuts and redundancies where we, through loyalties, have refused to take these options, and he may be able to solve problems which we cannot solve. I agree his demands are monstrous, but to use an army expression, there's no need for him to consider the enemies' feelings or their wishes once they have surrendered. I admire your stand, Lionel. The terms are onerous, but the alternative to capitulation is bankruptcy. Now, are there any other comments?"

He looked towards the production director, who said, "I'm not family, but I've spent my working lifetime with this company. What will my position be?" Harold Denton, at sixty-three, was no longer concerned over the future of the company, he was only worried about his own future. Would he be retained as an employee? Highly doubtful!

Richard Hemmings answered, "All pension plans will be honoured."

"Of course," said Denton, "but how about the golden handshake?"

"As I told you previously, there will be no handshakes – gold, silver, or brass!"

Denton exploded, "But that's unfair! I read in the paper the other day that the chairman of a company making heavy losses still got substantial compensation when he was asked to leave. Of course, he'd been clever enough to get an agreement signed while he was still in charge. We should have had similar agreements."

Donald Linklater said, "Brennan has made his position clear, and it wouldn't matter whether we had agreements or not. He believes that if a company fails it is the management that is at fault, and they should not be allowed to prosper from their inefficiency. "But," his voice softened, "Bob Brennan has assured me that he will do his best to look after our work force, although there will be a few redundancies."

"It's disgraceful!" shouted Lionel Linklater. "We've worked our butts off for the company, and we get nothing!"

Richard Hemmings again contemplated the scene. Donald Linklater showed so much commonsense, while Lionel, overpowered by his own emotion, showed no sense whatsoever. Yet Lionel had been responsible for most, if not all, of the problems that had arisen.

Because he had been so emotionally caught up, Lionel had obviously misled the Board again and again, and the chairman was perhaps too old to have resisted his nephew's claims as he would, most certainly, have done in his younger days. But Lionel was on his way out, and was only trying to make this last stand to impress his uncle.

There were further discussions, in which everyone joined except the financial director.

After a while Donald said quietly, "I think we have talked enough. We can't risk bankruptcy, which would tarnish the Linklater name. My wife and I, and our two daughters, hold the majority of the shares . . ."

Before he could continue Lionel interrupted him. "Uncle," he said, "you must not give way to blackmail!"

Donald, interrupting in turn, said, "Don't use such ugly words to me, Lionel, there is no blackmail." Then, turning to his financial director, he added, "Richard, is there, at this late stage, any alternative?"

"No," said Hemmings firmly. "If we continue trading, we could all be committing a criminal offence. Soon there won't be enough in the kitty to pay wages, let alone creditors."

"Very well," said Donald Linklater, sitting back in his chair, "we, as a family, will sell all our shares to Brennan, and I shall advise any other shareholders to do the same. Now let us take immediate steps to implement this decision . . ."

2   Enter Bob Brennan

The palatial offices of merchant bankers Scott & Ballinger reflected their standard and wealth in the eyes of the city.

The banking house had been founded after the Napoleonic wars by an emigré from Austria. In the 1920s the bank was first merged with, and subsequently taken over by, Scott & Ballinger, an enterprising and more modern group of merchant bankers. It was Stewart Scott, grandson of one of the founders of the group, who had put together the most recent financial package to bail out Linklaters. Now his reputation as a shrewd banker was at stake. He was determined on a quick and profitable solution.

Scott, an accountant, had served his qualifying time in the company of Richard Hemmings, and had recommended that Hemmings should join the Linklater Board. When it became clear from Hemmings' report that the salvage task was beyond the capabilities of Linklaters, Scott sought an alternative solution – and that solution lay in the person of Bob Brennan.

Brennan, at thirty-eight, had developed a knack of turning failures into winners. At twenty-eight he had joined the loss-maker Shepney Machine Tools, and had turned that company into a highly profitable group within three years. But all he had received from his drive and efficiency was a heavily taxed salary and a few perks.

It was then Brennan decided that that would be the last time he would make a fortune for other people.

Realising the potential upsurge in the demand for computers – the microcomputer age was just beginning – he opened a number of computer shops. He was first in the field. When the boom really got under way and competition became intense, Brennan decided to capitalise on his achievements and sell out. His company had been bought by a national group in the retail television field wishing to expand in other directions.

Married, a millionaire, and retired at the age of thirty-three, he rapidly came to the conclusion that to live happily ever after he would have to return to business. There was no contentment for him either in living on a yacht off Cannes or lounging around his luxury house in Sunningdale.

Once more he began researching for a new outlet. He travelled throughout Europe and the Far East, looking for a service or product whose need was not being satisfied by British manufacturers. Finally he discovered that there was a market for fractional horsepower motors. Through the Scott & Ballinger bank, which had first financed his computer business, he was able to make contact with a manufacturer whose managing director wanted to retire. After only a month's negotiation, Brennan bought the business and turned a relatively small company into one of the leaders in its field.

One of the reasons for his achievements in the fractional horsepower motor market was due to a customer – Brian Moss of NuAire Ltd, manufacturers of air-conditioning equipment. Moss had been one of the pioneers of quality standards, and his enthusiasm for quality control was contagious.

Very quickly Brennan set up a quality improvement division. He believed that was the turning point which enabled him to win the confidence of contractors, manufacturers, and distributors throughout the world. Event-

ually he sold out to an Italian manufacturer wishing to
enter the British market.

Brennan became a multi-millionaire. The sale had
been completed only a few months before Scott's
approach to him. It came at a time when he was looking
for a new challenge and a long-term commitment. He
investigated Linklaters in depth and discovered weaknesses which he knew he could eradicate. He believed he
could turn the business round within eighteen months, if
not less.

At the time he was approached by Scott and
Hemmings Brennan had decided that for him there
would be no more buying and selling of companies. His
main reason for this decision was that he wanted to build
a great business so that his son, Simon, then aged five,
could eventually take it over and prove himself to be a
worthy successor to his father. He was sure Linklaters
could provide the vehicle that would enable him to reach
his objective, but he knew that he would only buy on his
terms, which would have to be tough, even harsh.

Brennan's dictum was that inefficient directors
deserved to fail and should not be compensated for their
failures, they should be penalised; while successful and
efficient executives deserved generous backing. And
Brennan did not rate the Linklater family's efficiency
very highly.

The Scott & Ballinger boardroom area comprised a
main room and a reception area. The reception area
included a well equipped bar where, during meetings, a
barman was in attendance.

The boardroom itself did not have the conventional
table centrepiece for the directors to sit around. Instead,
there were comfortable chairs, each having its own small
adjacent table, which tended to create an informal
atmosphere.

The time was 9 am. Present were Stewart Scott and
Charles Ballinger; Sir Whitney Bowers, late of HM

Government and now chairman; the general manager of finance, Paul Lancotte; and the group credit controller, Arthur Mailey.

Bob Brennan was also present. He sat facing Sir Whitney Bowers, whose expressionless eyes and stern features had frightened many an adversary into a change of mind. But all the executives were experienced negotiators. They understood the 'give and take' formula – *give a little, take a lot!* Each of them could be tough when required, but not inflexible at all times. They all knew the strengths and weaknesses of Brennan – and Brennan was confident he knew the same about them.

Both sides appreciated that concessions should be held back – they might not be required. The board was determined to make Brennan work hard for any concession he wanted. They all knew how to bluff, and they knew that they had to maintain their tempers, unless they wanted to act a part.

Scott opened the meeting, saying, "We're all completely in the picture. It seems there are still a few points to be discussed which, I am sure, we shall easily sort out. But first, Bob, let me restate our essential requirements. After that, we can cover the bones of contention."

Brennan recognised the ploy for what it was – to minimise his demands so that they would sound of little consequence. Scott continued, "We are willing to accept Linklaters' equity to replace a part of our loan – that has to be negotiated. But our equity, Bob, must be 55 per cent, while yours will be 45 per cent. We will, however, agree to sell you our 55 per cent within a three-year span if certain requirements are met. You will know what these objectives are: reduction of the loan and a profitable Linklaters. This was all set out in the memo of intent.

"Bob, you will advise us of additional reductions in costs, and details of at least fifty redundancies, which we believe will be essential. The Linklaters Board will receive no compensation. With these conditions met, we shall grant the additional facilities to see the company through the transitional period.

"As there can be no collateral for this additional facility, we expect you, Bob, to give a personal guarantee. With these issues, I am sure you agree – they are beyond dispute." Then he added quickly, "But you raised some points of contention to which I am sure we can find compromise solutions. I'll begin with –"

Brennan held up his hand. "Stewart," he said, "You're going ahead too fast if you believe that I have totally accepted the memorandum of 3 April. You've been misled. Surely Paul told you that I don't agree with your decisions."

"I know, I know," said Scott. "Paul did make your views clear to us. But as an experienced negotiator you would inevitably disagree with some parts of our memorandum. You also know that there are fundamentals of banking which can't change, so why beat about the bush? We do have to move fast."

"I agree with you," said Brennan. "I also agree that you have banking rules which give you near as damn it one hundred per cent protection. But those rules didn't save you from the Linklater disaster nor, going back a few years, the collapse of the property market. Sometimes rules have to be broken, if losses are to be avoided. May I, therefore, make my position clear – because I don't agree with any of the points you have raised.

"(a) I will not hold less than 55 per cent of the stock; I want to be in control, not Scott & Ballinger. (b) I will not personally guarantee anything. (c) I will not agree to unnecessary redundancies. And (d) at the end of the first twelve months you will, if requested, sell to me or my nominees the shares you hold in Linklaters. And you will sell them at today's prices."

Sir Whitney Bowers said, "Mr Brennan, if you mean to stand by these decisions there is little point in discussing the future of Linklaters."

"As you wish," said Brennan, who at that moment felt the need of a cigarette, although he had given them up to please his wife. "It's entirely up to you if you wish to lose a few millions. There's nothing to salvage at Linklaters, as Parfitt & Clews have undoubtedly told you."

There was an uncomfortable silence, then Scott said, "What do you mean?"

"You know what I mean, Stewart. You instructed that well known firm of liquidators, Parfitt & Clews, to investigate Linklaters. You did so under the guise of seeking ways to give that company future financial help. They're a tough lot, and they would very much like to be appointed liquidators, but they did tell you that there was precious little that they could salvage from the wreck. There are no parts to sell off, no properties to turn into cash; their only real asset is a good name, and a potential to be highly profitable under new management."

Scott demurred. "I don't know how you have arrived at your conclusions. Parfitt & Clews were only carrying out a survey –"

"Liquidators rarely make surveys before they are officially called in."

"And how do you know all this?" asked Sir Whitney.

"Through questioning the right people, that's all! Ask the right questions, and you will, invariably, get the right answers. But it doesn't matter how I know. What does matter is that you now have a helluva decision to make. Either you liquidate the company and lose most of your investment, or you give me the backing I must have if I'm to risk my money and my reputation, by buying – and part-financing – Linklaters."

After further discussion Scott said, "Would you mind leaving us for a short while, Bob? The bar is open and –"

"Too early for me," said Brennan. "Don't be too long, though – I have a luncheon appointment."

Scott smiled grimly. He wasn't used to being pushed

around. He stood up and escorted Brennan to the reception area.

Thirty minutes later Scott asked Brennan to return. Sir Whitney Bowers felt confident of victory. His years in Government had taught him to sense impending victory over a colleague, a minister, or civil-servant militants. He had told the Board that Brennan wanted Linklaters as a business for expansion. He needed the name and reputation of an old established company; Brennan realised that he only needed to make the inefficient efficient, to cut costs, and to ride roughshod over suppliers, to succeed in his objective. Sir Whitney had emphasised that Brennan must be 90 per cent sure of success, or he would not be prepared to invest his own money. He had continued, "I don't make mistakes – I don't misjudge people. He is a typical tycoon, and I have dealt with many of them in my time. We've got him where we want him, you can be sure of that. We must have control; we must ask for his guarantees, to be certain that he doesn't milk the business."

Scott, not so sure, pointed out that Brennan was their last hope. He agreed with what Sir Whitney had suggested, but added a proviso.

"You won't need your proviso," said Sir Whitney. "We'll win!"

A relaxed Brennan returned to his chair, certain that he knew the attitude the Board would adopt.

Scott said, "Bob, it's make or break time. We've decided our terms cannot be changed in any substantial way, although we will consider minor adjustments." Unusually for him, Scott rambled on and on, and Brennan knew then that Scott was not happy with the Board's viewpoint.

When he had finished talking, Brennan said, "And that's final?"

"Yes – final!"

"Right!" Brennan stood up and said, "The oldest ploy

in negotiating is to pretend to leave – 'picking up the hat' as it's called – knowing that if it fails, one need only sit down again, and accept the best possible deal available. Well, gentlemen, I'm not bluffing. When I walk out of that door, the deal is over. I shan't renegotiate under any circumstances. I shan't attend another meeting. I shan't attend any private dinner in the hope of there being 'togetherness' again. The plan will be over – finished!

"Please don't misunderstand me, and don't misjudge me. When I made my position clear to Paul, I was not making the right negotiating noises, I was stating my definitive position. There it is, gentlemen.

"You wish to stand by your banking rules; I want to stand by my business principles, which have been successful in the past and which, I believe, could be successful again with Linklaters. But the going won't be easy. The decision for me was a hard one."

Sir Whitney Bowers said, "But Mr Brennan, you do owe us something, so surely we can negotiate. We backed you in your previous venture –"

"Sir Whitney, I disagree. You were not with the group at the time, but they backed me after demanding all sorts of guarantees. They wanted guarantees signed by almost everyone in sight. They didn't do me any favours – and quite rightly from their point of view. The Board was acting in the best interests of Scott & Ballinger. But favours? No!

"Now I'm acting in the best interests of Bob Brennan, and I believe the position is changed. This time I hold all the aces. But it's up to you." Brennan stood up.

Nobody made any comment as he walked to the door leading to the reception area. He entered the reception area, but just as he arrived at the door leading to the outside corridor he was caught by a puffing Stewart Scott.

"OK, Bob," said Stewart, "you win! But you can't blame us for trying. I did make a proviso, when the

Board were all in favour of a tough stance, that if the bluff failed, we would give way. We'll agree to 90 per cent of your requests."

Brennan smiled for the first time. "I'm glad, Stewart," he said, "I'm glad. You will save your investment – and I shall make another fortune out of Linklaters."

3 A plan for success

The atmosphere in the boardroom at Linklaters was very different from that prevailing when the directors had decided to sell their company to Brennan. Now there was an air of expectancy, excitement and, to some extent, fear. Around the boardroom table sat works manager Mike Spurling, sales manager Harvey Strong, general manager Laurie Wallace, service manager Victor Clayton, and financial director Richard Hemmings.

Sharp at 9 am the new managing director walked briskly into the boardroom and took his seat at the head of the table. "Gentlemen," he began, without wasting time on pleasantries, "you may well be wondering why I look upon you as our future management team, in view of the failures of the past. The answer is that after close investigation and grinding each of you through an interviewing mill, which was tough, wasn't it?" – they all agreed that "grinding" wasn't strong enough – "I don't think I can be certain of finding a better team, either by head hunting or advertising.

"It is usual in a takeover of this kind for most of the directors to be sacked. Well, that has happened in this case. The directors, with the exception of Richard Hemmings, have gone, but you were all acting under instructions. You were not given adequate backing and the changes you suggested were often vetoed, because of lack of funds. I see no reason, therefore, why Mr X, who may or may not have been effective in his present company, should prove to be a better bet for me than any one of you.

"At the moment the Board comprises me and Richard Hemmings, and two non-executive directors appointed by Scott & Ballinger to look after their interests. In twelve months' time, if we reach our objective, the two non-executive directors will go, and I shall be looking to replace them. Need I say more on this subject? Are there any questions, so far?"

Works manager Mike Spurling said, "There will have to be changes, obviously, but you haven't told us yet what these changes will be."

Brennan answered, "Think of the number of times in the past when each one of you has said something like this: 'If only they would listen to me I could do this or that, and things could be put right!' Well, I am prepared to listen to you, and make many of the changes you suggest."

No one spoke up, so Brennan continued, "But you will want to know of the changes I intend to make. Here are some of them. We shall close down the London head-quarters and all employees will be invited to move to Southampton; obviously, we shall help them financially. I am also going to close down all the branch offices – "

"Just a minute, Mr Brennan," said Harvey Strong, a bearded, six foot plus giant, "I'm depending on our area managers to initiate a renewed sales drive!"

"Of course you are," said Brennan, "and so they shall! But some of them will have to move. I'm determined that we stop selling in certain unprofitable areas. We shall concentrate on defined areas where we know we can get the business and we know we can operate our service maintenance scheme successfully. We're going to con-centrate on major industrial areas of the country only – but more about that later."

Service manager Clayton said, "But we shall still have to service all the other units in those areas where you are going to close area sales offices."

"I have the solution to that," said Brennan. "In all areas where it is too costly to service the units ourselves, the work will be carried out by Trex Ltd. Trex, as you may or may not know, manufactures lifts and garage doors. It found it extremely costly to give good service throughout the country – as did Linklaters. It overcame its problem by inviting other companies facing the same difficulties to allow it – Trex – to do this service work. It means that Trex engineers can be fully occupied in servicing perhaps three non-competitive products, whereas previously those engineers in the same area would only have worked part-time. The idea has proved a great success. I've been in touch with Trex and it's quite willing to undertake our service work. We shall have to train its personnel. Trex is expensive, but the cost will be small compared with the losses we were making in selling and servicing for ourselves in those areas.

"You must forgive me for my brevity but we have so much ground to cover. I do assure you that everything will be discussed and your opinions sought, at a later date. I assure you, too, that I've done my homework and I know exactly how we are going to turn Linklaters very quickly indeed from a loss-maker into a profit-maker."

Mike Spurling said, "I don't want you to think we're making excuses for ourselves, but we did suggest something similar to the late board, and the idea was vetoed."

Brennan nodded. "Linklater's rut was very deep!" He continued, "The next point is controversial. We are going to stop immediately all production of the computerised remote control unit – the seat of many of the serious problems. We shall also cut down the operational speed. Also, part of our difficulties with colour came through our determination to sell a smaller unit than our competitors. The size will now be increased."

General manager Laurie Wallace, plumpish, with pink

face which suddenly reddened, said, "But that's impossible! As general manager it was my job to oversee every aspect of the company's affairs – only answerable to the Board. I have been with the company since the inception of the copier, and I state categorically the main reason we were able to take on established competitors was because we had something different to offer. Harvey will bear me out on that.

"Every photo-copier company lists at least a dozen or more claims, ranging from speed of operation to clarity of the finished product. We offer the same dozen, but we couldn't have got off the mark without our own pluses. May I, with respect, put it this way, Mr Brennan. Have you ever known a relatively small company to take on a giant in its own field, having no price advantage, no service advantage, no advertising advantage, and no additional benefit to offer, and yet to succeed?

"It's always possible to pick up crumbs, but we're not looking for crumbs, are we?"

"I agree," said Brennan. "But the fact remains that the service charges to cover these special benefits were killers. We were, and still are, servicing some units almost every day. I intend to contact a number of our customers personally and tell them the truth – that until we find the answers, they should discontinue using the remote control unit, and our engineers will cut down on the speed of operation. To compensate them we shall lower the standard copying charge for twelve months. This, again, means losses to us, but it can still be less costly than maintaining the present position. I'm quite confident that I can persuade the majority of our customers to go along with my plan. It's surprising how reasonable people are when approached in the right way. Our sole objective at the moment is to win a large share of a flourishing home market, become profitable, pay off all our short-term loans, and then we can conquer the world!"

Harvey Strong interrupted. Brennan had already
learned that Strong was a difficult man to handle,
especially at meetings, where he liked to assert himself.

"Mr Brennan – " he began.

"Make it Bob – it's quicker. And that applies all
round."

"OK then Bob, our problem has been selling with our
reputation blown to pieces by our competitors. But we
didn't do too badly, and we're still selling in spite of all
the difficulties. You believe you can outsell others, and I
won't disagree with that, but Mark Cornell of Canada
Copiers is a real live wire. He's the one who is knocking
us most, and he's the one with a highly motivated sales
team. He's just taken twenty of their leading salesmen
and their wives to Miami. Now we have to beat him, and
to increase sales by cutting the sales force, and that
doesn't add up."

"It will all add up, Harvey. One of your mistakes" –
Strong's face flushed, and his beard appeared to be
jutting out even further – "was to diversify your efforts.
You wanted to sell in every nook and cranny of the
British Isles. I believe you once actually put it that way.
That, in my opinion, was a recipe for disaster. The cost
would have beaten you, even if the service department
had managed to cope. You tried to solve the problem by
decentralising, opening area offices. That is one certain
way of increasing costs. An office, which begins with one
manager, ends up with a secretary, a telephonist, and
ever-growing staff – and ever-growing overheads."

"That's not fair!" said Strong.

It was Brennan's turn now. "Harvey, when has life
ever been fair? If fairness had played any part, Linklaters
would still be a prosperous company. But please don't
let's get involved in detail. Just withhold your comments
until you have heard the whole story."

"You asked for questions," insisted Strong.

"True! But that was fifteen minutes ago. Now I'm

asking you to leave questioning me until later. Let me continue to outline our strategy. I promise you a series of meetings when every aspect can be debated. There are four objectives which, if achieved, will lead us to success.

"The first is cost management, and I have already indicated some major savings in that direction.

"The second is a sales drive in the limited areas which I have outlined.

"The third, a very strict quality control, so that never again shall we run the risks that Linklaters took when they began manufacturing the copiers. We have to win for Linklaters the name for top quality."

Sales manager Victor Clayton said, almost apologetically, "We have always striven for quality. Remember the only serious mistake we made was in going ahead too quickly on Lundt's patents."

"That is partly true," said Brennan, "but I think you will find, as our discussions proceed, that the quality was lacking in many other directions also."

Richard Hemmings said, "Bob, I'd like to refer back to what Harvey said. How can we obtain more business while we are reducing the number of potential clients?"

"Richard," said Brennan, "let me spell it out – and my belief is based on experience and past achievements. Linklaters won a fair share of the copier market, and that was quite an achievement. But the firm was only selling to a fraction of the market as a whole. We are not going to forget our duty to our customers, as I told you. What we are going to do is to ensure that a great many more office-appliance buyers will have the opportunity of purchasing Linklater copiers. Concentrating on a smaller, specific market, can do just that. The biggest time-waster for all salesmen is travelling time. We shall beat competition, as I have done before, because in so many of the giant organisations salesmen forget to sell, and sales managers forget to train their salesmen to sell –

they live on reputation. Our men are going to become the great persuaders.

"I have been told that selling is the gentle art of giving other people your own way. I promise you that we shall apply that dictum to the full."

Strong said, "I think I know a good deal about selling —"

Brennan again interrupted, "Please don't take everything as a personal criticism, Harvey. If we don't make changes there is no hope of survival, and if we don't motivate sufficiently there is no hope of survival. There's still a large untapped market; untapped, because no one calls on the buyers. Our competitors rely mostly on advertising to bring in the enquiries. We shall go out and sell while our competitors are still getting around to writing quotations. I know that one of our competitors sometimes takes a week — even longer — to answer an enquiry, and a further week to two weeks goes by before a salesman calls. That isn't quality selling — something we'll talk about later. We shall answer all enquiries the same day as they are received, and our salesmen will call within twenty-four hours. And this we can do, if we concentrate on smaller sections of the country."

Suddenly, his face softened and his voice changed. Smiling, he said, "I realise that at this moment you're not very fond of me. I'm an interloper, an interloper in an old-established company. That's fair enough! I realise you think that perhaps I'm in this business to make a quick profit and a quick resale of Linklaters, once it's built up. And I know you've all considered looking elsewhere for your futures.

"How do I know this? Because that's exactly how I should react under similar circumstances if I were in your place.

"Make any enquiries about me that you like and I think you'll find that I tell the truth, and I don't bluff my own staff. Believe me, therefore, when I say that I'm telling you the truth now. I intend, with your help, to build up this business. I do not intend to sell it unless unforeseen circumstances arise. I should like you, therefore, to reserve judgement for a while, and if I do let you down, you can then tell me what you think of me. Richard knows me fairly well; he knows that I still believe a man's word is his bond. I give you my word that I have meticulously worked out my plan for our success, and I am confident that it can be achieved if you give me your full support. Does that ease your minds at all?"

General manager Laurie Wallace rose from his chair, walked round the table, and shook Brennan's hand. "That's exactly what we all wanted to hear," he said.

"Thank you," Brennan said. "Now let us look again at one of our problems and its solution. Our aim is to win for Linklaters and its products a name for quality. Remember, our competitors' machines also break down and some don't give immediate service. My objective is so to improve our quality that we need give as little service as possible – in fact, I am now working on a plan which will result in the customer being paid if we should have to give them service. That is the sort of quality deal I'm seeking.

"Now I should like to talk generally about quality. Afterwards, we can have a discussion, and this will be followed by a surprise which, I think, will please you.

"It's generally assumed that quality control only applies to production, but that is not so. Of course, production does take precedence in quality assurance; however good the service department or the sales division may be, there is no future for a product that does not offer good quality in relation to the market requirements.

"There is, however, another aspect of quality. You can produce the finest product – our copier, for example, will soon be in that class – but if the back-up service does not also offer quality, the effect of the product quality will be negated. We must, therefore, have quality service.

"Unless one has a monopoly, even products of the highest standard, marketed at reasonable prices, will not sell themselves. We must, therefore, have quality marketing.

"Maybe at some time the old tag about the buyers queueing up for a better mousetrap was true, but it is not true any longer. The highly efficient marketing company employing its own professional salesmen will, more often than not, take an order away from a company claiming, truthfully, that it is making a 'better mousetrap'.

"Our objective must be high quality standards for every aspect of our business, from the shop floor through every department, right up to Board level. Unless we can make everyone a fervent evangelist for cost-effective quality – in the office, in the field, in the factory, on the telephone, when writing letters – it will be impossible to achieve our objectives. There must be quality by example, and a better quality of life for all our employees.

"When, from now on, I refer to a *quality manager*, I do not necessarily mean a production quality controller, but any manager of real quality with all-round ability. An outstanding manager has to have that special quality which is so easily recognisable by all personnel, including the managing director."

He began speaking more rapidly as he warmed to his subject. "Quality," he continued, "does not mean luxury. It only entails working to set standards, and these standards should apply to every walk of life. This is an extract from the *New York Times*." Brennan began reading aloud from a cutting. "It is headed *Cabbies' Ties Pay Off* and the copy reads:

"Cab drivers in San Francisco have found that those who smarten up and clean up, wearing a shirt and tie, and looking less like an unmade bed, are worth a lot of dollars a week in takings. This was discovered in a two-week experiment by the Yellow Cab Company, when a dozen drivers were asked to wear ties, shirts, jackets, short haircuts, etc. Their earnings were compared with another dozen tee-shirted, unshaven drivers. The average takings of the spruced up drivers during the two-week test was $1600 compared with $1040 of the 'dirty dozen'. One of the drivers, when asked for his comments, said succinctly, 'It's quality, see? We look good – the cab looks good – so the customer feels good.' "

"A good example," said general manager Laurie Wallace, "I don't want to cap it, but may I tell a 'quality' story?"

"Of course!"

"My brother is a director of Swann Packaging. He told me that his company decided to switch to electronic typewriters with memory banks, etc. He asked his secretary to try out several models and let him know the results. First, she telephoned a company advertising a typewriter at about £500. I won't mention any names, because Jack might not want me to. The machine was delivered by a supposedly trained representative, but he explained immediately to the secretary that he was relatively new with the company and, therefore, not able to explain fully the ramifications of the typewriter. He left her to discover the benefits for herself – which she found some difficulty in doing, because the instruction manual did not clearly set out the capabilities of the typewriter, nor how it should be operated.

"For three days the secretary tried, unsuccessfully, to master the techniques. She telephoned the suppliers and asked for advice, and two days later an expert arrived, full of excuses because he was three hours late for the appointment. He began the teaching session, but five minutes later the machine broke down. The expert assured the secretary that this was most unusual, but that he'd arrange for a mechanic to call. Three days later the

mechanic arrived – also one hour late for his appointment
– and fixed the machine. A representative then telephoned to ask if he could borrow the machine for an
urgent demonstration, and said he would return it the
following day. The machine was not returned until ten
days later.

"The secretary telephoned to cancel the trial, and told
them to collect the machine. It was not collected until
four weeks later. That, Bob, I am sure, is what you mean
by bad marketing quality."

Brennan was impressed by Laurie Wallace. His
example had been told with conciseness, and emphasis in
the right places.

Brennan said, "Laurie, one question: how would
Linklaters have acted in similar circumstances?"

"Bloody badly!" came the reply.

"Hey, wait a minute," said Strong, "as sales manager I
object to that statement."

"You needn't, Harvey," said Wallace. "You always
did a good job. You did your best to train everyone with
the faciliites available, and you helped your salesmen all
you could. But I could see what was going on in the
office."

"Why didn't you do something about it, then? You
were the general manager."

Wallace shrugged his shoulders. "I don't want to
blame anyone, and Bob knows our problems. But Lionel
Linklater would never listen to critics, and he kept
cutting back on staff, so that juniors were dealing with
enquiries. You must remember I was not directly
involved with the sales department – I was more concerned with general running of the offices."

Brennan said, "It would be salutary if managing
directors were sometimes to check on their sales departments. But let's forget the past and concentrate on the
future. We have stressed the fact that quality applies to
every aspect of the business.

"Brian Moss of NuAire Ltd summed it up in this memo to his employees:

The manner in which a telephone call is answered and directed.

The speed with which a quotation is prepared, and the accuracy, appearance, and completeness of that quotation and its supporting information.

The relevance and tone of letters.

The appearance, competence, and enthusiasm of the sales engineer.

The keeping of delivery promises and the attitude of the carrier.

The efficiency of the sales order department, the service engineers, the accounts personnel . . .

Everyone in a company is responsible for the quality of that company.

There can be no argument about our products – after all, we have, justifiably earned the BSI mark, but what about our service?

How do YOU rate in the Quality Stakes? How is NuAire thought of as a result of your contribution?

Would the BSI award YOU a mark because they were convinced they could consistently ASSURE clients of YOUR quality?

Brennan paused, then said, "Why do you think I am encouraging stories that prove quality pays? We all claim to be quality minded, so why gild the lily? The reason is that nearly all firms – the bad, the indifferent, the good – claim that they believe in quality, but their enthusiasm is quickly dampened if a problem arises in output or a salesman moans that the competition is tough. I want to prove the case for quality, so that we never again let expediency enter our minds." Brennan sipped from the glass of water and studied his colleagues. He knew it would take time to win them over.

There was diminutive Mike Spurling, known to the

work force as the 'darting' man – he seemed always to be
darting here, there, and everywhere. He had blue eyes,
fair hair, and at forty-one was in his prime.

Harvey Strong, in his mid-forties, looked tough with
his bristling beard and imposing appearance. But was he
tough – or was it all bluff?

General manager Laurie Wallace, at forty-seven, over-
weight through the enjoyment of good food and wine,
did seem to have a good brain. Or was he just a poseur?

Then came service manager Victor Clayton, tall, thin,
balding. At thirty-six he was a manager with a lot of
potential.

Next to him sat Richard Hemmings, a difficult man to
understand. He had an ice-cold brain and apparently a
total disregard for the criticism of others. An excellent
finance manager – but could he be trusted? Did he ever
give his loyalty to anyone? Brennan wondered . . . Then
he continued, "I want each of you to consider every
aspect of your work, and how the quality can be
improved in your own department. But even this is not
enough. This is the era of the multi-discipline manager,
and to improve quality overall it is essential that we all
learn more about the disciplines of other managers in our
group.

"Do your homework quickly. Research as much as you
like, but you all have to be ready for a meeting which will
commence within four weeks, and will cover every aspect
of high quality management."

He smiled brightly and said, "And here's the surprise:
We are going to hold the meeting on board the QE2,
which sails for the USA in four weeks. And I hope your
wives will accompany you."

The faces of the management team mirrored their
delight at the idea.

Brennan went on, "A gimmick, some will say. A
show-off by a show-off, my detractors will declaim.
Possibly! I think differently, however. This is the

beginning of a new, dynamic era for Linklaters. Another reason why I want us to be together so closely is so that we can all get to know each other better. To succeed, we have to work as a team. On board ship we shall work very hard, but there'll be plenty of time for relaxation as well."

Everyone suddenly was clapping hands, applauding the decision of the new chief executive.

Later that day one of the managers telephoned Mark Cornell of Canada Copiers.

4 A problem of relationships

Vivienne Brennan, busily packing, said, "Are you sure you're doing the right thing? Remember the problems at our office parties with men displaying their machismo in front of their wives? It will be worse on the ship, when we'll be together not for three hours or so but for five and a half days. I'm dreading it!"

Blonde, blue-eyed, with beautifully chiselled features and a figure of a fitness fanatic, Vivienne was adored by Bob, who also respected her views. "You could be right, Viv," he said, "but I'm backing my judgement. I've got to find out a little more about them – what goes on behind the façades. I must know the heavy drinker, if there is one. I must know whether their wives will be prepared to back them during the gruelling days ahead. I must know how a man will behave when relaxed and not putting up a pretence, and I must have the opportunity of driving home my message, again and again."

"I hope it works out for you," said Viv.

Harvey Strong was not in a good mood. He had asked Bob Brennan if he could bring his girl friend with him. They had been living together for eight months, since his divorce had been finalised. Brennan had readily agreed, but then the trouble had started.

The girl friend, Pat Moore, refused the invitation because of what she called her invidious position. How was she to be introduced? Common law wife? Ugh! Girl friend? Horrible! Fiancée? If she were his fiancée, that would be different . . .

When the romance had started, they had both agreed there were to be no obligations except that of respecting each other. But it had not worked out that way. After some six months she began insisting that maybe it would be best for both of them if they were married, and had children. Harvey didn't want to be married again so quickly. He was quite happy just to have a loving girl about the house.

The problem, simmering for a couple of months, had blown up again when he had given her the surprising news that she could accompany him on the QE2. Misguidedly, he had thought that she would be overjoyed at the very idea of a voyage to the USA. For all his size and bluster, Harvey was not really tough, and in the end he had grudgingly given way and agreed to a wedding two months later. He did not so much mind marrying Pat as he did the thought of giving way to her ultimatum. He, Harvey Strong, the great persuader, the great salesman, the great charmer of people, had quit.

How often, when lecturing to his salesmen, he had said, "If you haven't the guts to fight on and obtain the business, you should get out of selling. Selling is synonymous with persistence." And he, Harvey Strong, had crumpled up when Pat went into one of her tantrums and refused to sleep with him, saying she would walk out unless the decision was made immediately.

As time passed, however, he began to feel better. He knew Brennan, for one, would fall under Pat's spell. Everyone did, and maybe that would be all to the good.

Laurie Wallace was quite confident that his wife would captivate Brennan. She was Brennan's type – resolute of character with strong opinions and a good general knowledge of subjects from sport to politics.

Dorothy was delighted at the thought of spending five

and a half days with the Brennans. She was as certain as her husband that Brennan would quickly look upon her as an exceptional woman – unlike Pat Moore, who was bound to be empty-headed; or Mary Clayton, who was so dull; and Penny Hemmings, so boring about her country life. She only wished Laurie had a little more drive, more determination to succeed. She was proud of the fact that he had qualified as a barrister before moving into business and, subsequently, joining Linklaters.

Victor Clayton was a compulsive worrier over detail. He also believed in having alternatives. He was, in fact, a 'braces and belt' man, but his foresight – or obsession – did mean that he made very few mistakes. He had done well to keep the service going under most difficult conditions.

He saw his future as a director of planning, at which he was so good, rather than as a service manager. His wife, Mary, had only two ambitions: to be a good wife and to make a success of bringing up her four children. She was not widely read, and had only a slight knowledge of sport, politics, or current affairs. But she could talk endlessly about babies, or cooking.

When Mike Spurling had told his wife, Tina, about Brennan's QE2 plan, she had said immediately, "I haven't a thing to wear!" Then she had added, "If Dorothy Walllace starts putting on her airs and graces act with me, I shall tell her a few home truths."

Wincing, Mike had said, "Please, Tina, please – no quarrels, no arguments. Go and buy yourself some dresses if that's what you want."

"It isn't as easy as all that!"

Then followed a discussion on the difficulties of getting the right clothes for the occasion without time to look around.

Tina, small, dainty, with large brown shining eyes

said, "And another thing, Mike, I never quarrel with anyone unless someone upsets me."

Mike had wanted to say, "But someone is always upsetting you, and often, it is because you are so tactless," but he kept quiet. He knew he could not win an argument with Tina, mainly because he hated upsetting her.

Since their son had gone to boarding school, she had worked as a computer programmer. In a business discussion she would be able to hold her own with anyone, but the risk was that she could easily lose her temper, and he hoped she wouldn't with the Brennans.

Penny Hemmings had qualified as an accountant before she married Richard, but had given up practising when Richard had inherited some capital on the death of his father. They had bought a farm with a manor house, and Penny and Richard enjoyed playing the squire and his lady in the village of Downton, in Kent.

Buying the house, redecoration and furnishings had used up a fair amount of the bequest, but that didn't worry Penny, although it worried Richard. Penny enjoyed organising fetes, helping charities to raise funds, and serving on a marriage guidance council. She could be warm and extremely friendly to those she liked, and very, very cold to those whom she considered did not show her the respect she felt she deserved.

"Oh dear," she said to Richard, "what a bore! What an unutterable bore! I don't think I can stand five days of that Wallace woman, or listening to Mary Clayton telling me about her children."

They bickered for a while, then Richard said, "OK, if you don't want to go along, I'll make an excuse for you."

"Oh no, you won't," said Penny. "Then you'll blame me if things don't work out. You always do. I'll come, but I shall hate every minute of it."

5 On board the QE2

Stewards were pushing luggage-laden trolleys, lights flashed outside cabins as passengers called for the assistance of their steward, and voices could be heard – some commanding, some pleading. "One of my cases is missing, steward." "How do I adjust the air-conditioning?" "What time does the hairdresser open?"

Brennan and Vivienne sat in their cabin, relaxing. Coffee had been brought to them by a stewardess who had willingly found the time to serve them, even although she and her steward partner were under extreme pressure. The cabin was luxurious – pastel shades of pink and cream walls, with matching covers, curtains, and upholstery. All the fittings – lights and switches – were gold-plated. On the verandah there were deeply padded deckchairs.

Every few minutes the telephone rang. The callers were the managers, reporting their arrival. Bob gave each a warm welcome, enquired as to their and their wives' welfare, and informed them: "Lunch is served from one o'clock onwards. Tables have been reserved for us in the Queen's Grill, and the afternoon will be free, so that you can settle in. I've arranged to take over a part of the computer training centre, and we shall all meet there at six-thirty this evening for a general discussion. If you make for the upper deck and walk down the passageway on the port side away from the shops, the meeting room

is straight ahead of you. Do bring your wives. Drinks
have been laid on."

At six-twenty-five Brennan and his wife were waiting
for his team. He guessed that they would all arrive
together, and they did. The first to walk towards them,
hand outstretched and smile overstretched, was Dorothy
Wallace. Dress for the evening was informal, but she was
wearing a most expensive, sleek-fitting brown Dior
dress, while her husband wore a complementary dark
brown suit. Following the general manager and his wife
were Harvey Strong and Pat. Brennan thought she
looked stunning in a green trouser suit. She had dark
hair, greyish-green eyes, and the shape of a model,
which, indeed, she was. Strong was still wearing his
tweed travelling suit.

Vivienne noticed the soft sexy look that Pat flashed at
Bob.

Harvey said quickly, "Just to let you know the good
news – the others know it already – that we're getting
married in two months' time."

"Congratulations!" said the Brennans in unison.

Following them came the Claytons – Mary, plumpish,
looking a little flustered, wearing a black dress because
she thought it right for the occasion; and next, the
Spurlings, almost bustling in. Vivienne liked Tina
straight away. She had that indefinable charm which
quickly won people over.

The Hemmings arrived looking, they thought, like the
typical country squire and his lady. He wore a Savile
Row tailored brown blazer with a yellow tie and fawn
trousers. Penny was wearing her travelling suit – she had
not changed, either. It was a two-piece from St Laurent
of Bond Street.

In the room Brennan had organised a well stocked bar,
and a steward was in attendance. Soon they all had a
drink in their hands. After some thirty minutes' chatting
Brennan said, "I don't want to spoil the party but I

should like to have your attention for a few minutes. I am sure you are all eager to know the agenda for the next few days.

"As far as our wives are concerned, there are no arrangements; they can do as they wish and I'm sure they will all enjoy carrying out those wishes. I'm afraid it's different for us," he went on, putting on a sad expression. "We menfolk have to work hard for a living – well perhaps not too hard. I'm sure we shall all find it enjoyable.

"There will be several separate sessions each day, commencing at nine am. Lunch, as you know, will be served in the Queen's Grill from one o'clock, and we shall have to be there on time. By the way, if you only want a light midday meal, you can enjoy salads, etc. on the Lido deck. The afternoon sessions will start at about two o'clock each day, and finish between five-thirty and six. It would be rather nice if we could all meet for drinks in the evenings in the Queen's Grill bar at, say, seven-fifteen to seven-thirty, and we can dine about eight-thirty. From then on, your time will be free, and you can mix or not, just as you wish. You can gamble in the Casino, watch the cabaret, play bridge . . ."

He paused to sip at his drink, then continued, "Now gentlemen, for the details of the first session. Tomorrow will be devoted to *People Management*. Each of you will make a contribution. I'm quite certain you have all done your homework. I shall give you the programme for days two, three and four later. Now, are there any questions?"

"What happens if we're seasick?" asked Harvey Strong.

"You go to the doctor and he'll give you a jab; but you still turn up on time!

"Now, let's go in to dinner."

6 Quality in management

All was well. Everyone had been on their best behaviour over dinner, although Brennan did notice the warning glance from Dorothy Wallace when the waiter refilled her husband's wineglass for the fourth time. At the other table, Pat's vivacity was not at all affected by Penny Hemmings' constant endeavours to prove her sophistication. Penny studied the wine list and discussed the various vintages with the steward. She had regaled everyone with stories of the many famous restaurants she had patronised in Florence, Paris . . .

After dinner they had gone their separate ways, but however late they had been retiring to bed, all the men arrived punctually on time for the first session the following morning.

It had been decided that dress should be informal. Wallace looked immaculate in fawn jumper and dark brown and yellow spotted shirt, with matching cravat, while, at the other extreme, Harvey Strong wore crumpled jeans and a heavy woollen sweater.

The men were seated in a semicircle, facing Brennan, who began. "The principles of People Management apply equally to the manager of a small shop employing five or six assistants, and a ship like this with nearly a thousand crew members. Cunard believe that the quality of the QE2 depends solely on *people*, as it does for us at Linklaters. The managers on board have to originate, watch out for stress, justify change, and arrive at decisions without the help of immediate back-up teams, such as we have in industry. Although the QE2 crosses the Atlantic in five and a half days, many of the ship's company may have been away from home for several weeks.

"We all know of the petty grievances, foolish arguments, and grumbles, which take place in our own offices and factories. Our employees, however, do go home at nights, and can let off steam then, or rid themselves of their frustrations by gardening, house decoration, or golfing at weekends. On board ship relaxation areas are provided, but they cannot possibly take the place of the local pub where everyone can solve other people's problems in a friendly atmosphere.

"The QE2 management, therefore, faces daily problems, and its objective is to ensure that no problem affects the enjoyment of the passengers.

"That, gentlemen, is what quality means." Brennan paused, then said, "You may smoke if you wish; I've given it up." No one smoked.

"So long as we remember," he went on, "that the rules of managing people apply to *all* managers, everywhere, we at Linklaters can reach our objective of high quality management. Managing a shop-floor worker or a transport driver, office staff or salesman, is no different from managing a waiter, an engineer, or a steward. The rules of people management never vary."

Brennan looked directly at each of the managers in turn, then said, "Each of us will contribute to today's session on people management, but there is one point before we begin. You will all agree that probably the most important function of any manager is to motivate others. We need not discuss this at length; motivation deserves a special session on its own, and this will be on Thursday." He paused, then continued, "To have high quality products we must have a high quality production

manager – and that, for the time being, has to be you,
Mike. Our marketing strategy must be well ahead of our
competitors. Harvey, you are our high quality sales
manager and I shall now consider you as acting marketing manager."

This statement pleased Strong immensely, although it
did not have the same effect on the others.

"We must be sure," Brennan went on, "that Linklaters will never again be over-extended, and in the hands
of our bankers. We have a high quality finance manager
in Richard Hemmings to take care of that. We must be
certain that our administration is all that it should be.
For quality administration we have a general manager –
you, Laurie. And finally, the person with the most
difficult task, possibly, is Victor Clayton, who certainly
has to be a high quality service manager.

"How do you rate yourselves? It's so easy to use the
word *quality*, but we have to live up to it, don't we. Some
believe that the way to discover the truth about ourselves
is to be appraised by senior executives. At such appraisal
meetings we are led to believe that the person being
appraised is quite happy to be criticised and may say, 'I
didn't realise I talked too much,' 'I really did think I was
a good administrator,' or 'I realise now that I have to
reduce stocks . . .'

"All this is sheer nonsense. None of us can really
accept such criticism, because we don't believe it to be
true. Remember, what those being appraised tell their
executives is not the same as they tell their associates and
families. That is why some executives, and others who
are praised, believe appraisals to be so remarkably
successful.

"I believe we can only put things right if we can
discover for ourselves weaknesses we are not prepared to
admit to others.

"How can we learn to admit these truths about
ourselves? It's impossible unless we have the inner

strength to admit that sometimes we take wrong actions which may be of benefit to us but not to the company, that we sometimes make instant decisions to show our authority, that we take time off for the wrong reasons, that we believe an idea is a non-starter purely because we don't like the originator of that idea . . .

"Do we really believe that we are always right and others are always wrong? Do we really care for our employees? Or do we put on a sanctimonious act to impress others?

"The only people who believe they are perfect and always right are the militants, fanatics, and thickheads – and we can do nothing about them!

"But reasonable, thinking people can apply the cure, which lies in the *Does it apply to me?* tests. Let's try some; if we can't use these self-tests then this session is a waste of time. We will begin," Brennan went on, "by considering what, possibly, our employees think of us. To them are we *if only* people? For example:

"'*If only* he would tell me where I can contact him. . .'

"'*If only* he would learn to dictate, and not umm and ahh so much . . .'

"'*If only* he would understand that I, too, have a home life . . .'

"'*If only* he would stop blaming others when he makes mistakes . . .'

"'*If only* he would realise that a twenty-year old typewriter is not as efficient as an up-to-date word processor . . .'

"'*If only* he would stop complaining when I am a little late, while he takes two or three hours for a so-called business lunch . . .'

"'*If only* he didn't keep everything to himself. . .'

"'*If only* he would stop throwing his weight about in public . . .'

"'*If only* just now and again he would say sorry . . .'

"'*If only* he would insist on the full facts before deciding who is right . . .'

"'*If only* he didn't have favourites . . .'

"'*If only* he weren't so dogmatic . . .'

Brennan paused, then said, "Well, that's not a bad list to begin with. How about some self-criticism now. Let's pause for thought, and I invite you to supply more *if onlys*."

After a few minutes Strong said, "I know what they say about me – '*If only* he kept a tidier office, he wouldn't complain so much about me losing his letters and papers'."

This caused general hilarity. They all knew it to be true, and were surprised to hear Strong admitting his weakness. He was well known for claiming, "I know where everything is!" Suddenly, they all wanted to get in on the act.

Wallace said, "'*If only* he wouldn't use ten words when one will do!' Surely that proves I'm using the *Does it apply to me?* test!"

More applause! Brennan knew they were accepting the criticism as well as directing it towards themselves – again proof that most people will, on occasion, admit their weaknesses, but will fight very hard indeed if those same weaknesses are pointed out to them by others.

After some moments' thought Spurling said, "There has been criticism of me in the past which I couldn't accept. Perhaps I was wrong. Let me put it into the *if only* category. '*If only* he would not take so long to ascertain all the facts and then, when he has them, seek even more information and then begin all over again before arriving at a decision.' Maybe," Spurling said, "I do that to delay making decisions; I'll have to think about it."

Everyone knew that one of Spurling's weaknesses was his reluctance to make decisions or take immediate action.

Clayton said, "'*If only* he would stop delegating the checking of engineers' expense accounts to others. They sometimes get away with murder.'"

"Do you mean that?" asked Brennan.

"Yes, and I'm only admitting it now because Richard discovered what was going on and drew my attention to it. And Richard was right. My engineers soon knew that joyride was over!"

Brennan said, "How about a final one from Richard?"

Hemmings answered, "Nothing for me to confess. I'm perfect!" He was greeted by boos.

Brennan thought, what matter? We're all children at heart.

Hemmings went on, "Thank you for your friendly greeting. Now I must make my point clear. I can't quote an *if only* because, as financial director and chief accountant, I am criticised by everyone. The Board eagerly awaits the monthly management accounts, but if the profits are not high enough, they dispute every figure and believe I am distorting all the facts. When costs rise, I am to blame for not pointing out the misdemeanours of others. When we decide that it is right to withhold payment of accounts for as long as possible for the benefit of our cash position, I am criticised by nearly everyone. The production manager can't get his supplies, the office manager can't get his stationery. When we reverse the procedure and pay our accounts promptly and make a drive to get our money in quickly, the sales force is up in arms, complaining bitterly that we are upsetting their customers. Even if a salary increase is not up to expectations, we share the blame with the managing director. So you see, there are so many *if only's* so far as I am concerned. Does that satisfy you?"

"Not really," said Spurling. "Some of the *if only's* are justified, because, once again, a financial director makes excuses like everyone else. They hate admitting that they could possibly have made a mistake. Maybe you should listen to some of those *if onlys*, Richard. Maybe there is some in between action that could be taken, rather than upsetting either production or sales."

Hemmings said, "Possibly you're right; but it's best if the financial director is not the most admired man in the company. Too much back-slapping might prevent him from producing the right figures for the right reasons at the right time."

Brennan smiled, and it was the kind of smile that made girls say, "Isn't he lovely!" and men think, he's not so bad, after all. He said, "Now let's consider the manager's relationship with his managing director. How can the managing director help to improve his managers' skills, quality, aptitudes . . . ? Who will begin? Please speak your minds. I confirm there will be no instant dismissals!"

Ready laughter again – and again relaxation. Brennan knew that relaxed people are more apt to speak their minds than tense ones.

Wallace said, "Forgive me in advance, Bob, for this one. I'm not referring to you, but some managing directors resent being told anything. Why is it that if a managing director thinks of a new concept, it is always perfect and bears no contradiction, while if a manager approaches him with the same idea, the answer will probably be, "I'll think about it", which means that the idea will be turned down. Is it psychological? Do managing directors really believe that they know it all? I'm exaggerating, of course, but I do make a plea for the managing director to take advice more readily from his managers."

"You're right again, Laurie, I agree. You are all seeing the best side of me – the worst is yet to come! How about you, Richard?"

Hemmings said, "Once more I'd rather be left out. If I think of anything, I'll let you know."

"And you, Victor? What do you object to in a managing director, which may hinder managers from becoming managers of quality?"

Clayton hesitated, then plunged in. "From my past experience every managing director claims, as you have done, that he doesn't want 'yes' men around him. But is this true? Managing directors do have favourites, and they're usually those who tend to agree with them. They're apt to talk to them about associates who may be more difficult, and this can frustrate capable managers, who may perhaps not so readily agree with their chief."

"That's a good one," said Brennan, "and it's so true. And I can't claim that I'm not guilty of favouritism – or even prejudices against some people. But any managing director who allows his personal feelings to affect his judgement is not worthy of the position."

"Thank you," said Clayton, who knew that sometimes he was awkward and not too popular with top management, while everyone admired and liked Laurie Wallace, who never seemed to put a foot wrong.

"Any other comments?"

There were none, so Brennan said, "Then let us now consider some aspects of management in which you may be deficient. Who'll make a start?

Hemmings said, "There is one requirement of management which is lacking in many executives. I make a plea for all managers to have a greater understanding of finance. Too few of them can fully understand a balance sheet or a profit and loss account – they know little of the effect of a negative cash flow, or what gearing means. There was a plea earlier for the managing director to listen more to his managers, but how can he listen carefully when so much of the action requested by managers necessitates the spending of money – new this, new that, increased expenses, bigger cars. I once knew a manager who thought that the cash balance at the end of the year was the actual profit. Incredible, isn't it? The finance of rentals is little understood, and the danger of over-trading can so easily be avoided by anyone with financial knowledge.

"I appreciate the subject can't be covered in an hour or so, and anyway, Bob, it isn't included in the agenda so far as I know, but may I make a plea that all managers throughout the group either make a personal study of finance, or attend an outside course – or, to save money, I'll run a course for them."

"I agree with that one hundred per cent," said Clayton. The others also nodded their agreement, so Brennan said, "Richard, your idea will be implemented. You make the necessary arrangements. May I suggest that in view of the pressure on your time we use an outside course?"

Harvey Strong said, "I agree with Richard that we all need a better appreciation of finance and accountancy, but I think it's second in importance to the need for managers to understand salesmanship."

"God forbid!" said Wallace. "We're not salesmen."

"That's a typical response," said Strong emphatically. "If, twenty years ago, a bank manager had been told that he must learn to sell, he would have resigned if he could have afforded to. The word was anathema to all bank managers. Then came credit cards and managers were asked to enrol as many of the retail customers as they could in the scheme. One bank sent its managers to an outside sales course, although it was called a *seminar on negotiating*. Just semantics to save the dignity of the managers.

"Nowadays, all managers sell – whether insurance, finance, or banking. But they still prefer to think they are negotiating rather than selling. The reason why so many salesmen don't get the backing they deserve is that managers haven't any idea of what salesmanship entails.

"There was a letter in *The Times* recently from a British importer working from Singapore. He asked the

question: 'Why is it that we can get immediate response
so far as prices and quotations are concerned from
companies in nearly every country except Great Britain,
where four or five weeks is the average time – if we're
lucky!'"

Wallace interrupted. "Just a minute, you're going too
fast. Bank managers, insurance managers, finance
managers – yes they do sell these days. But Mike
Spurling doesn't have to sell and neither do I. And as for
sending out quotations, surely that comes under the
heading of administration rather than salesmanship."

"You're quite wrong, Laurie, 100 per cent wrong! You
and Mike sell all the time."

Brennan said, "Harvey, I agree with you. But the
others don't, by the look of them. You can have an hour's
session on Thursday or Friday, to persuade them that
every manager is a salesman. Will that do?"

"Thank you," said Strong. "That's just what I wanted
to hear."

Spurling said, "Possibly it is right that we, in production, should know more about the problems facing
Harvey's salesmen, but shouldn't he learn more about
our problems, too?"

Before Strong could answer, Brennan said, "You are
right, Mike. That is why all of tomorrow will be spent on
production problems."

After some discussion Wallace said, "What about
human relations – the right way to influence people? Are
we having a session on that?"

"I don't think so," said Brennan.

"Oh dear! Why not?" asked a surprised Wallace, who
really did try to live up to the tenets of human relations.

"Because," said Brennan slowly, "the carrying out of
human relation practices depends almost solely on commonsense." He paused for effect before continuing, "I
don't believe you can persuade people to keep to the
principles of human relations. You can list them, then

hope for the best. But it all comes down to commonsense, and that is a very rare commodity indeed.

"If, for example, an exasperated manager loses his temper and starts ranting at a member of his staff, he will, at least, know that he is acting incorrectly, even foolishly. Everyone knows he is wrong, but commonsense sometimes disappears when emotion takes over.

"It is commonsense to give praise where praise is due, because praise is a great force in winning people over, but if a manager lacks commonsense, he can be told what he should do, but he still won't do it.

"It's commonsense not to criticise people unless it is necessary to do so; and even where it is essential, it should be balanced by a measure of appreciation. But if a person lacks this sensibility, he may learn the rule but he will still forget that *it does apply to him*.

"It is commonsense to be well mannered. It is commonsense not to put on a pompous, masterful act just because you're a manager. It is commonsense that you can only talk tough if you hold the right cards and know how to play them. It is commonsense not to kowtow to the strong, and to help the weak. It is commonsense to apologise if we are wrong, and commonsense to listen more and talk less . . .

"You see, Laurie, I think everyone here knows the tenets of human relations, and we all employ them from time to time; but at such times as our commonsense disappears, the human factor disappears as well. I don't know how much commonsense each of you has, but whether you can always practise human relations in business is a matter of your own personality, background, and of course, commonsense.

"I try to practise it and, possibly, I succeed 70 per cent of the time. It all boils down simply to acting towards others as we should expect them to act towards us if our positions were reversed. Does that answer your question as to why I don't believe that we need to devote an hour or so to talking about human relations?"

Wallace smiled. "No wonder they call you brilliant, and I'm not kowtowing! You've covered the many aspects of human relations – indirectly, you've challenged all of us to carry out the tenets and to prove that we are not lacking in commonsense. And you are possibly right. We can teach people to speak well in public, to write better letters, to master skills and techniques, but a man has to discover for himself the great value of the ability to influence people by acting towards them in a manner which reflects his understanding of human relations."

"Thank you, Laurie, let's all try to appreciate that value," answered Brennan. "Now if there are no more points of contention I should like to end the session by highlighting the difference between an average manager and a *high quality manager*. We'll make a game of it. I'll give you the reactions of *Mr Average*, and you give me the reactions of *Mr Quality*. Here we go.

"He works assiduously at continuation of the status quo."

The immediate response from Strong was: "The *high quality manager* must always look for new opportunities for the benefit of the company."

"That's a good start," said Brennan, "but it was an easy one. Here's another.

"He considers changes are not within his province – they are the sole prerogative of 'those upstairs'."

Again Strong reacted quickly: "The *high quality manager* believes all changes are challenges. If he inaugurates a change which doesn't, at first, seem acceptable, in spite of rebuffs he will keep stating his case, providing more and more facts, and hoping he will win through in the end."

Laurie Wallace broke in, "This isn't a game, it's simply a means of providing Harvey Strong, who has such a quick mind because he has spent a lifetime in selling, with an opportunity to impress all of us with his talents."

"That's true enough," said Strong nonchalantly. "In the world of selling, every salesman has to have a lightning mind. But I've known you to be pretty quick on the uptake on many occasions in the past, Laurie."

Brennan put a stop to this discussion, interrupting with, "Well here's another. He is disconcerted by unexpected problems when they arise."

Wallace got in quickly before Strong could answer: "This ties in with one of my favourite maxims: *A manager should never be surprised – never shocked.* This simply means that he can read the signs aright. He can foresee problems that might arise at some time in the future. Whenever he gives an instruction, he will know if there are likely to be any future difficulties. Therefore, he is never surprised if work gets behind, for example, because he has made arrangements to tackle the problem in that event."

The managers were now all straining to be the first to answer the next question.

"Here's another easy one," said Brennan. "Mr Average loves systems, detail work, report forms, believes in confirming every instruction, and, of course, he is a memo man."

Richard Hemmings said, "You're talking about me again, Bob. I admit I have always been a paper man. I have always felt the need for everything to be confirmed, every instruction detailed, because there are so many fools around. There has always been too much paper streaming out of the offices, in case someone should forget a verbal request. My letters were always two pages instead of one. I insisted on stock sheets for checking stock sheets.

"I owe it to Old Man Linklater for curing me of that! When I instigated a cost-cutting drive, he told me the story of how Marks & Spencer cut their paperwork by 70 per cent, and that no one was the loser. He told me that I couldn't expect everyone else to cut costs while I was continually wasting so much paper."

"And he was right! Putting it into your words, Bob, the *high quality manager* doesn't believe in too much paper work."

Spurling said, "And I used to be on the receiving end of it. You should have heard what I used to say about you from time to time!"

"I can imagine," said Hemmings, with a smile.

Brennan said, "Let's all take a leaf from Richard's book. Anyone else want to make a confession?"

Wallace said, "I used to believe that everything should be structured, with a step by step approach. That stemmed from my legal background. A structured interview was, I believed, essential. There should be a structured typing pool, no rule should ever be broken, all meetings should be structured. But I am no longer a completely structured man. Do you know why?"

Brennan answered quickly, "Because structuring so often kills initiative as well as the fun in business – and there can be fun in business, the excitement of innovation, the joys of breaking a rule and still succeeding . . ."

"One hundred per cent right!" answered Wallace.

"I'd like to raise a point," said Clayton. "The average manager seeks security first and, therefore, avoids taking chances. True, or false?"

"True!" said Strong. "The high quality manager derives his security from his knowledge that he can do the job better than anyone else."

For a moment there seemed a sense of unease among the managers. Brennan said, "That's true, but there is no real security for any of us. As Harvey said, the only security is that which we make for ourselves. I, for one, would never blame anyone for taking a calculated risk – that is one of the assets of the effective manager. But there's little security for the manager who takes risks at the expense of his company without being able to validate those risks.

"The belief of such managers can be summed up in these words: *They've got plenty of money, profits are good, so what if it does go wrong?* But let's get it straight. None of us can succeed without taking a calculated risk from time to time, but the question we should ask ourselves where finance is involved is, *would I take the same risk if I were using my own money?*

"Now let's have a final one."

Spurling said, "It's my turn. The average manager is often prone to side with his staff, especially if he has risen from the ranks. He is constantly aware of the fact that before he was promoted, he often criticised the company, he often bent the rules. Now he has to tell his subordinates that they must not bend those very rules.

"The rule should be that a manager of high quality will always take the part of the company during an argument. Later he may discuss the matter with top management, and if he can persuade them that the subordinates are right, he can return to his men and admit that perhaps a mistake has been made. But he can't be one of the boys and the manager at the same time."

Brennan announced a short break, as a steward had arrived with coffee and biscuits.

7   Managing stress

After the coffee break Brennan said, "Mike, I know you want to talk about stress and its effects on the work force and manager."

Spurling was quick off the mark. "To me," he said, "a most important factor in quality management is the management of stress and change. I worked closely with Victor on this subject, and I should like to cover stress as a factor in quality management – and Victor will show how stress and change are integrated."

Spurling waited for a nod from Brennan, then continued, "I'm sure we all know that quality always suffers when someone is under stress, but so often we are not aware of the stress we cause. A memorandum from the chief executive can cause stress for managers; similarly, a memorandum from the managers to their staff can be a stress-maker. Why? Because, usually, most memos instigate some sort of change – put this right, do that, make sure that deliveries are on time, stop breakages, instigate new rules about pilfering, justify expenses, and so on. Changes have to be made.

"When first the memo is sent out, the recipient recognises from the envelope and the typewriting on it where it has come from, and that in itself brings about instant stress, even before the envelope has been opened."

Brennan said, "But how else do we communicate,

especially when we want several people to receive the same information?"

"And that," Spurling answered, "is often another stress-maker. The recipient knows that colleagues will be reading an implied criticism of him. Well, Bob, we had such a bellyful of memos at Linklaters that everyone got shaky about them.

"I cut memos by 90 per cent. And restricted them to 'information only'. Any criticisms were given orally, and only confirmed in writing where absolutely necessary. It worked wonders."

Hemmings, a confirmed memo-writer said, "I disagree. Memos are an essential business practice."

"Informative memos, yes, I agree. But there is little need for memos when a change is necessary, or when there has to be criticism.

"Talk, talk, talk, and we short-circuit so much controversy, because when we talk, explain, we can smile, shake hands . . . A memo can't do that.

"I know this doesn't apply to you, Richard, but so many memos are sent to show authority."

Before Hemmings could start an argument, Brennan cut in, "You need not continue; we're here to make decisions on quality, and you've made out a case.

"You'll receive very few memos from me in the future." Then he added, "But Mike, you're not telling me that memos are the main cause of stress?"

"Of course not, but sometimes they are a contributory cause. They are linked with change, and always affect quality. Here are eight other stress-makers which should be imprinted on our minds:"

"Before you go on," interrupted Wallace, "may I make a point?"

Spurling, annoyed at being interrupted in full flight, hid his feelings with a smile and said, "OK."

"Mike," said Wallace, "aren't you making a mountain out of a molehill? We all suffer stress on occasion, we all worry from time to time, and what is the difference between worry and stress? Surely stress affects so few people that it's hardly worth giving it priority. This, after all, is only our second session on People Management!"

There was silence for a moment, and Brennan looked quizzically at Spurling, who had obviously tensed up. Then Spurling relaxed and said, "Worrying is akin to problem-solving. When Harvey, for example, is concerned about falling sales, he may worry, but because he is a capable sales manager he isn't under stress. The worry or, as I prefer to call it, problem-solving will continue until that moment arrives when Harvey can say perhaps, 'That's it! That's what I'll do!' and the worry ends. But stress doesn't disappear so easily. Maybe there wasn't so much stress years ago, but you've only to be on the production line for a few days to know how ordinary, decent, working people can so quickly succumb to stress. And under stress people make all kinds of statements, make all kinds of mistakes – and foolish faults occur.

"Worry overcomes problems, stress doesn't. Stress saps the will and the mind. Refuge may be taken in drink or illness, and, sad as it always seems, the sensitive people suffer most from stress. If we want a quality organisation, we must be prepared to make change after change, and this is what I am leading up to.

"All big changes cause stress, with the possible subsequent temporary loss of skills, drive, and ability to cope with work. Does that answer your question, Laurie?"

The ex-barrister said, "I'll have to think about that!", which was typical of him. Everyone laughed, and the tension was again broken.

Spurling continued, "Now for my eight points, and after that I'll give you my views on how to recognise these signs of stress:

1. Stress is caused when someone is overloaded with work he doesn't like doing, or is given tasks he is not

capable of completing efficiently. These people are invariably the *willing horses*, who never refuse to undertake any task. But although they may seem calm enough when accepting it, they suffer from an inner turmoil and stress. We all know our *willing horses*, and we mustn't take them too much for granted.

2. Never hint at promotion if there is the slightest doubt about the hint being turned into reality. If we make such semi-promises, the recipient can hardly get home fast enough to tell his wife the good news. She tells her friends, "I think Frank is going to be made a manager soon, isn't it wonderful!" Then if he is not promoted within the reasonable future, he will be under stress as he finds excuse after excuse for this lack of promotion.

3. Fear is a great stress-maker, and all threats cause fear. A threat could be implied in any almost casual statement – "You know the boss is very tough on those who don't reach their targets." What can *tough* mean, other than being sacked?

   Stress is also caused by fear of the unknown – *How will it affect me? Shall I be found out? Shall I be able to cope?* All that is necessary is for the manager to make the 'unknown' known.

4. When someone in an office, shop, or factory, feels 'out of it' – has no rapport with colleagues – that person may come under stress.

   If someone is the victim of prejudice – race, religion, or sex – that person may also suffer stress.

   It is up to the manager to be observant, aware of what is happening, and determined to put things right. Often a friendly talk is all that is needed.

5. Technological changes can cause stress, much of it unnecessary. The fault usually lies with management not taking the work force into its confidence. There is

all the difference in the world between *consulting* and *negotiating*, and too few executives *consult* – which may lead to tough *negotiations* later.

6. Often a person blames his work for stress when it is only a substitute for the real cause. Arriving at the office grey of face, bleary-eyed, he is told by well meaning colleagues that he doesn't look too good and must be working too hard. If a person is told this often enough, he will begin to believe that it's true. The real cause of his stress may be wife trouble, a child, or some other family problem.

   Managers should aim to build up such a rapport with their team that the member under stress will confide in them and seek advice. But even if the problem seems insoluble, a heart-to-heart talk can often help the person to live with it.

7. If an employee commits a misdemeanour but is not worried about his wrong-doing, he won't suffer stress. If, however, he has a conscience which keeps pricking him, he will develop an anxiety, leading to stress. These stress problems sometimes apply to those who are away from home for long periods.

   A man knows that he should not let his wife carry so many home responsibilities, but, against this, he enjoys drink, good food, and travel at the company's expense. Eventually, if he has a conscience, he will be under stress. This can also be allied to overdrinking, a widespread problem these days. Unfortunately no one ever recognises the symptoms within himself, and this can cause untold misery and stress.

   Managers should always keep close checks on subordinates who spend time away from home. They should be able to sense when things are going wrong. One sign is when someone always wants to visit a certain area, or country, when there seems no apparent need for such regular visits. Often this is a

sign of enjoyment taking the place of business objectives.
8. Stress often occurs when somebody genuinely has more work to do than he can cope with. The cause may be an upsurge in business, depletion of staff, or, in the case of service managers, too frequent breakdowns of machinery, with customers telephoning continually for immediate service.

The upsurge in work, if temporary, rarely causes problems, except for the not so capable *willing horses*. It is when it becomes continuous that it causes stress. However, this is often the easiest situation to cure, for all that is needed is better time management and spreading the work load. Time management, which, of course, includes delegation, will often save someone from succumbing to stress."

Spurling paused for a moment, then asked, "Any questions?"

There were none, so he continued, "Here, then, are stress symptoms which we must all strive to recognise:

1. If a person suddenly begins to cover up mistakes.
2. When a usual steady gazer avoids looking you in the eye.
3. When someone who usually arrives at work in spite of colds, coughs, backaches, or strikes, develops virus infections, backaches that become slipped discs, headaches that turn into migraines, and for whom temporary hold-ups in traffic become major build-ups with traffic trailing back for miles. These can all be stress signals.
4. When someone stays in his office for long periods; ostensibly working hard, he is possibly fearful of new demands. This can be a stress symptom.
5. When someone who is not a regular complainer starts complaining about the clicking of typewriters, loud

talking, the constant rattle of teacups, bad seating, bad lighting, bad air conditioning, etc.

6. A lowering of standards. Under stress, concentration is hard to maintain, but without concentration standards fall. A person under stress spends most of his time thinking about the problems which are causing the stress.

"These are only some of the symptoms. As managers, you must have understanding, patience, compassion, and a desire to bring out the best in your team. We can only do this if we watch for warning signals and then talk the problem through with the person concerned."

"Well done!" said Wallace. Then added, "Mike, you're a works manager looking after some 500 employees. Do you practise what you preach? And how have you become so knowledgeable about the problems of stress?"

Spurling said, "Because of my concern at the stress caused by management I attended a course with Victor which taught how to handle change and stress. Quite frankly, I've quoted a great deal from their notes. I'm sure Victor won't mind me telling you that his talk will probably also be based on that course."

Clayton, who had made up his mind not to say anything about the course they had attended, smiled weakly and said, "I was going to mention it."

Brennan said, "It doesn't matter where the information comes from. There's nothing like practical experience such as both of you have had, allied to the experience of others in the training field."

Spurling concluded, "That's all I have to say on the subject. I'm sure there will be discussions and helpful contributions."

Brennan shook Spurling's hand in a congratulatory manner, which, again, did not please either Wallace or Clayton. He said, "We must all remember that People

Management is solving many small problems. There are only a few large ones."

The discussion which followed lasted some time, until Brennan announced that there would be another short break.

8 Loyalty

During the break Brennan said, "I must make a 'phone call. I'll be back soon."

Hemmings said, "Problems?"

Brennan nodded. "There are always problems, but I believe they are coping well, all things considered."

After Brennan had left the room, Wallace said, "Even at this early stage Bob seems to be the type of leader who inspires loyalty."

Strong disagreed. "I don't go much for this loyalty guff. What is loyalty, anyway? Paying lip service to the Guv'nor – yes sir, yes sir, three bags full! We've got to face it, loyalty has died out. Bob Brennan can't expect loyalty from us. I'll work myself into the ground, not for Bob, but because I'm built that way. I can't do less than my best and I don't want to let the team down; but loyalty – whatever that may mean – no!"

"You do, then, believe in loyalty," said Wallace.

Strong looked puzzled. "How do you make that out?"

"You said you do your best not to let your team down. Isn't that loyalty – loyalty to the team? And if you're loyal to the team, indirectly you are being loyal to Bob. In fact, if you're here in five years' time, Harvey, we might even substitute the word Bob for the team."

Strong said, "Well, putting it that way –"

Wallace interrupted, "There is no other way. To me loyalty simply means allegiance to someone or something deserving of our love, affection, respect. Our Queen, our country, and also those who employ us, provided they care for our welfare and show a sense of responsibility towards us and, therefore, win our allegiance. If that's the way Bob intends to act towards us, he will command our loyalty, which only means that we shall be willing to go that extra mile for him."

Strong said, "You should have stuck to the Bar. You put your case like a typical barrister. But at the moment we can't be expected to show loyalty, as you put it, to Bob."

"Why not? Why not give him the benefit of the doubt that he will act responsibly towards us, that he will also go the extra mile for us? It isn't guff, Harvey, it means a great deal to many people."

Spurling said, "You're not suggesting, Laurie, that loyalty, allegiance, call it what you will, means that we must never opt out, never emigrate – offer our allegiance to a new country? Even the most loyal Yorkshire cricketer might decide that he'd be better off playing for a southern county."

"Exactly!" said Wallace. "Loyalty only means a special relation with a unit, be it county, country, or a work-shop. It never means that we should not leave a company to better ourselves. No one would ever condemn that! It only means giving that little bit extra and, possibly, not running down those who employ us."

Hemmings said, "Would loyalty mean to you, Laurie, not leaving a company suddenly if it would jeopardise that company's future? Does it mean that none of you would leave Bob today if someone were to make you a most generous offer?

"I'm not committing myself on that." said Wallace. "It would all depend."

"You mean it would depend solely," said Hemmings, "on what the offer was worth; whether someone who doesn't like taking risks feels he might have more security by not leaving. If you were approached next

Monday by a head hunter offering you a position of managing director plus security, plus additional perks, would you say 'no' because of the loyalty in advance that you're suggesting we have for Bob?"

Wallace said, "That's a hypothetical question. It can't be answered."

At that moment Brennan returned. "We've made a good start," he said, "let's have an early lunch."

The ladies joined the menfolk for drinks in the Queen's Grill lounge, except for Pat, who had decided she would rather cut out lunch and spend more time in the Golden Door spa. The aerobics and the water exercises appealed to her – she had a dread of putting on weight.

Brennan noticed the speed with which Wallace downed a gin and tonic, while Harvey Strong seemed satisfied with a tomato juice. Penny Hemmings asked for a very dry Martini, and then complained that it was not dry enough. Not to be outdone, Dorothy Wallace had a Scotch on the rocks, and insisted that the whisky must be Bells; which seemed a waste of time to Brennan, because all whisky on the rocks tasted the same to him.

Each of these little scenes was observed by Brennan, to be used later in his final assessments.

9 Managing change

The afternoon session began at two-fifteen. Laurie Wallace knew that it had been foolish of him to have a couple of large gins before lunch, and he had noticed the look on Brennan's face when, over lunch, he had asked the waiter for a glass of red wine. He had also noticed that Harvey Strong was not drinking at all, and neither was Mike Spurling. He knew, too, that later he would be lectured by Dorothy.

Brennan said, "It's your turn, Victor."

Clayton began, "Last evening I attempted to pay cash for my drinks but the bar steward told me that it was signed chits only, with settlement at the end of the voyage. The reason was obvious, but I asked him the general reaction to this innovation.

"He replied, 'First, we blamed them for introducing a time-wasting idea; then we blamed them for interfering with our tips. Then we all agreed that it wouldn't work, anyway.'

"I suggested that it was working, nevertheless, and he said, 'Yes, actually it works very well. You see a service charge is included now, so we're all better off'. And that," went on Clayton, "is a typical example of the effect of change. First, there is resentment, then certainty that it won't work, and finally acceptance, if the change proves to be for the better or has no great effect on the individual concerned. What we have to determine are *ways to stop resentment building up in the first place*, as we shall be making many changes, particularly in the near future." Looking at the erudite Wallace, he went on, "Laurie, how about these two quotations for starters? The first is from Machiavelli: *There is nothing more difficult to carry out nor more doubtful of success, nor more dangerous to handle than to initiate a new order of things.* And secondly from Newton's Second Law of Motion: *For every action there is, equally, an opposite reaction.*

"I see that Laurie can hardly credit how learned I am. I must be honest, both these quotes were given to us at the course I attended with Mike. But they do sum up the situation whenever change is introduced.

"Possibly the main reason why change is rejected is that we see it as a threat to our security. Even a change of office or the introduction of a new computer can cause a feeling of insecurity. In addition, there is the shock of the change. So many executives dramatically announce a change when there should perhaps be a gradual build-up. The work force doesn't like shocks.

"Finally, none of us minds a change so much if we have taken part in its planning, or our advice has been sought. We can then explain to others the objective of the change, when it will take place, who will be involved, what the long-term effect is likely to be and, probably most importantly, how it will affect the individual. Can it cause loss of earnings? Discomfort? Inability to grasp the implications? Fear? We have to bear in mind all these possible stress-makers, and try to explain them away."

He paused, and Brennan said, "That's a good opening, Victor – well done!

Clayton smiled wanly and said, "I'm afraid you're not going to like the next bit as much, Bob. You've said that no one likes criticism, but do you, Bob, think you're blameless in the way you have inaugurated the changes you have decided on? The first Harvey heard of our new sales policy was at the London meeting. The first I heard that we were going to employ outside service contractors was at that same meeting. We all know you have a reputation for being a tough negotiator and a rapid decision-maker, but don't you think we should have been consulted before these announcements were made? As I mentioned earlier, consultation and involvement are very important in change. Am I speaking out of turn?"

"No," said Brennan. "Your criticism is justified only because you don't know me very well. I came to those decisions after most careful investigation, thought, and reasoning – after distillation of all the facts. I wanted the decision to be mine so that neither you nor Harvey would have to explain to the sales or service engineers that it was partly your decision which would result in some redundancies."

Clayton said, "We all appreciate your thoughtfulness, but, again, I hope I'm not speaking out of turn when I say this is the kind of excuse used by all managing directors when they want to make a decision without allowing anyone to argue about it. You may have considered the viewpoint of the work force, but did you consider our point of view? May I explain, and then you can decide if your policy was the correct one."

Brennan thought both Clayton and Spurling were already talking like main board directors. He said, "Carry on – I'm glad I'm not surrounded by 'yes' men. The worst that can happen to the 'no' men is that they get the sack!" He laughed and the others joined in, so that once more the tension was eased.

Clayton said, "Following your announcements we were nearly all anti, which we might not have been if there had been prior consultation. We were no different from the barmen. You said there would be discussion subsequently, but would you then have steam-rollered us into acceptance?"

"Just a minute," interrupted Brennan. "Remember the notice on President Truman's desk – *The buck stops here*. The same applies to managing directors. Sometimes a managing director has to make a tough decision, and he can't allow for any consensus of opinion."

"That's right," said Clayton. "But I wasn't so much thinking of the important decisions perhaps as of the hundreds of minor changes which are also made by managing directors without consultation. And surely there are very few important changes which are not deserving of some form of consultation other than that at main board level. It is the people who have to carry out the changes who should be informed before the decisions are made. On those rare occasions, however, when a sudden change has to be put into immediate effect, surely a full explanation should be given to the manager, who could, in his turn, pass the message on. There seems such a wide gap between the main board and the management team. Yet, if I may say so, it is the management team that has to implement all the changes to be made."

Brennan said, "You are now in the realms of decision-making, but I do see your point. Shall we leave it at that? The decision is now made that there will be more consultation on my part before the directives start to be stacked in the in-trays – no, wait a minute, I mustn't do that! We have to cut down on memos, haven't we? There's a lot that I have to remember," he concluded with a smile.

He was a little concerned at the way the session was heading. He didn't want conflict with his managers in these early days, yet he could sense that he had made a blunder. He had told them at the time that there would be consultation before implementation, but that was obviously not good enough. He went on, "And there will be no steam-rollering, only gentle nudges. But again I do want to emphasise that on these far-reaching changes I shall be willing to listen to amendments before the new plans are implemented."

Everyone clapped, and Brennan knew he was off the hook.

Clayton paused before continuing, "Forgive me for carrying on the discussion so far as consultation is concerned, but that is what change all boils down to, if it is to be acceptable. Recently, I read an article in a catering magazine on the changes made in an hotel. They had three general managers in almost as many years. The first decided to change the china in the magnificent dining room. The restaurant manager at that time said, 'Why, oh why didn't they ask me about it? I could have saved them the money. We had that new china about six years ago and gave it up because it was too fragile. It looks very nice but costs a bomb to replace.'

"The second manager decided that most of the main dishes were to be cooked at the tables by waiters. Special trolleys with spirit lamps were provided. Again, the restaurant manager said, 'That lasted about six months. Some of the waiters weren't capable of doing the job properly. There were a couple of small fires; the chef left because he was so upset about the arrangement, and in our lovely restaurant there was a constant smell of cooking, because the air conditioning was inadequate to deal with the fumes. There had been no consultation. The guv'nor had been to a Paris restaurant where, he said, it had worked like a charm, and everyone liked to see the flames. What he had not realised was that that was a very small restaurant, where the patron did most of the cooking at the tables himself. We can seat eighty people at a time, so there were never enough trolleys, and everyone was kept waiting. What a flop!'

"The third chief executive, when he arrived, decided to refurbish the dining room. He said customers should enjoy a closeness, so he decided on semicircular banquettes. They looked very attractive, but they took up so much space it almost halved the seating capacity in the room. And when the tables were full, the waiters were having almost to throw the plates across the tables in order to serve those sitting at the centre of the semi-circles. Again, the restaurant manager said that the designers had never even shown them the plans. If they had, they would have been told that it couldn't possibly work.

"Once more I ask your forgiveness for repetition, but at the course Mike and I attended it was driven home to us that only by repetition would we, as managers, ever be made to remember that we have to consult our teams just as much as the main board should consult us.

"And that is my case for consultation completed."

Everyone agreed that Clayton had made his point.

"Then the next factor I must deal with," went on Clayton, "is fear. Mike has already explained how fear causes stress, but so far as the change is concerned, there could be fear of failure when a change is announced. There could be two thoughts in someone's mind: *Can I do it?* and What will be the result if I fail? But that same person would never have the courage to tell his fears to others, or to his managing director.

"When told of the change he will probably say, 'Sure I can do it. No problem!' although to his associates he will condemn the change, rant against those who have made it, and suggest that it's almost impossible to carry out. And all because he is fearful of the results.

"What, then, does the average manager do when instructed to effect a change which he feels is wrong, and which he is not capable of seeing through?

(a) He can resign; but that's a non-starter, unless he has another job lined up.

(b) He can develop a psychological illness, which will be real enough to him.

(c) He can delegate the task, so that someone else gets the blame if it goes wrong.

"What the main board has to do so far as we are

concerned, and what we have to do so far as our staff is concerned, is alleviate this 'fear' aspect of the change. From our point of view we must be certain that when we delegate, the person asked to undertake the task is capable of doing it."

Clayton breathed deeply, having temporarily run out of breath. Then he continued, "There is another aspect of fear, and that is fear of the unknown. And that, Bob, could be our fear. You are unknown to us. We only know that you have a reputation for drive and toughness, and that you have been highly successful. You may well say that if we have confidence in ourselves, we have nothing to fear. I accept that, and I'm not admitting that any of us have such fears, only that it is a possibility. Now I can imagine how the work force feels. Everyone, Bob, is suspicious in advance of changes they know you will make.

"If we don't install new equipment we are old-fashioned. If we do, what is our ulterior motive? Some will wonder if they are being downgraded, others, if they are capable of mastering the new techniques."

"What's the answer to that?" asked Bob. "Do we have to interview everyone before we make a change? It seems to me that we're back to consultation again."

"No, not everyone," said Clayton. "If it is fear of the unknown that is troubling certain people, the sooner the reasons for the change are explained, the better. I appreciate that in the main I have been rather negative – what we must *not* do. I feel that I should now finish on a more positive note. Perhaps I could enumerate some of the points I have in mind:

1. If we feel we cannot tackle a task, admit the truth to ourselves and to others, but then make a determined effort to learn and develop the skills necessary to carry through the operation successfully. It is, after all, a challenge to us as managers.

2. When minor suggestions are made and we don't know whether they are right or wrong, let's carry them out. They are rarely costly, and we lose nothing by testing. We can lose the respect of others both above us in the hierarchy and below when we dismiss changes out of hand.

3. There are going to be many new arrivals at Linklaters within the next year or so, and every new arrival is a cause for concern. I'm quite sure that you, Bob, said as soon as you bought Linklaters, 'There will have to be changes!', and not before time. But having said that, you will be met by others who will tell you, 'We've tried that before and it doesn't work'.

   "This is a nonsensical answer, because nothing is static in business. Changes that were a failure when made one year can be successful later on. When I mentioned the problem of the hotel earlier, the criticism there was that advice had not been sought, not whether changes should have been made or not. The new ideas could all have been adapted to better purpose. All of us have used that excuse 'We've tried it before'. We must be careful about using it in the future.

4. We managers sometimes feel resentment against change which we should have thought of ourselves and, therefore, when a subordinate suggests such change to us, we immediately criticise it. This is wrong.

5. We are for change when we inaugurate the idea ourselves and become emotionally involved; then, invariably, we attempt to persuade others that we are right. We accuse those against of being reactionary, frightened, too old, rut-bound, and not forward looking. If we are young, we wonder whether it is worth while working for such traditionalists – joggers, who never want to change speed. If we are older, we indict the youth of today as incompetent

and anti-change because they don't have the ability to see it through. Our subordinates make similar accusations against us, when we turn down their plans for change.

"That, then is my message. From now on when pressing our claims for change or having change thrust upon us, we know why we are pressing for some changes and resisting others.

"Bob, I'm sure you can rely on all of us here to be objective about changes in the future, as we can rely on you to keep to the rules of change."

As soon as he had finished speaking there was a burst of applause, and Clayton felt well pleased with himself.

Brennan said, "Well done, Victor. Now let's have a ten-minute break."

10 Managing conflict

After the break Brennan said, "Now it's Laurie's turn. He wants to talk about *managing conflict*, and *how conflict can affect the quality of an organisation.*

Wallace began, "Once conflict has started, dislikes turn to hatred, and it may be a long time, if ever, before a more reasonable relationship can be restored.

"This is the message which should be imprinted on the mind of each of us:

"*Think* before we act.

"*Think* of the other person's reactions.

"*Think* of the possible conflict which may result.

"Unfortunately, many managers are so preoccupied with their own problems that they are never aware of the problems of others until conflict starts.

How are you? is usually a perfunctory, meaningless question, because the person asking it doesn't mentally register the answer. The reply may well be, "I have another dreadful cold because no one will ever shut that outside door!"

"Later, there could be conflict between the person worrying about the cold and those who will not shut the office door.

"An observant manager knows instinctively when something is wrong. If he is used to being greeted with warm, friendly smiles on entering the general office, and one morning he becomes aware that the smiles are missing, he knows something is wrong. Later he will send for one of the office staff and try to discover what it is so that he can, if possible, head off conflict. But a manager who is unaware of what is going on around him will never notice a different attitude in the staff, and will be shocked when told that someone is leaving because . . .

"Here are other warning signals:

1. When someone stops having lunch in the canteen with other members of the staff.
2. When there is constant bickering among the staff. This, on the face of it, can appear to the uninitiated to be jocular teasing, but often it is not. At some time or another someone will make a remark which will cause conflict. Bickering is a definite warning signal.
3. Conflict can be caused by the formation of cliques. Such cliques in offices or on the shop floor can lead to conflict.
4. A high staff turnover is a definite warning signal.
5. A change to which there has been strong opposition, but which is forced through, can cause conflict.
6. An increase in absenteeism due to illness.
7. Favouritism on the part of a manager usually leads to antagonism on the part of the other workers.
8. When anyone has been given an assignment that is beyond his capabilities, he will develop an antipathy towards the assignment and will try to form a faction to back him.

"It is not always necessary to act immediately on noticing the warning signals. Sometimes it is right to do nothing and let matters settle down. But a good manager must be aware of these, so that he can decide whether appropriate action is necessary.

"There are also conflicts between departments in companies. A manager knowing the inevitability of such conflicts must do his best to minimise them by being fair and objective, and not taking sides. For example, a director who is closely associated with sales will almost invariably take the part of the sales force when a conflict arises over quality control or bad deliveries. If, however, the director himself is an engineer, and has his head-quarters at the factory, he will almost always side with production. He will emphasise to the marketing director that he, the marketing director, knows very little about production and that is why he is always making unfair demands.

"What we, as managers, have to appreciate is that some of these conflicts are inevitable, but most can be forestalled by demanding facts, not generalisations, before giving a ruling.

"The rule for minimising conflict, therefore, is: *Step in early, before those involved harden in their attitudes and then resist every attempt to show that they could be wrong.*"

Wallace sipped water, then continued, "What are our options when we have not been able to forestall a conflict? We are then confronted with A disagreeing violently with B.

"Before concentrating on the options available, we must first obtain all the relevant facts, if possible from independent sources, as well as from the disputants. We shall then be able to identify the problem.

"It is no use seeing A and then, later, B without having all the facts available, because A believes himself to be completely right and will slant his evidence to prove justification for his condemnation of B. But when we see B, he will act in exactly the same way, and will prove that right is on his side.

"When all the facts have been collected, we can then decide on our options, which are:

(a) Send for A and discuss the matter with him.
(b) Send for B and discuss the matter with him.
(c) Wait for things to blow over.
(d) Try to calm things down in a general way.

(e) Call a meeting.
(f) Discuss our options with other managers.
(g) Make up our mind quickly, and sack either A or B, or transfer them to other departments.

"The option we shall probably decide upon will be to see A and B separately. At these meetings standard techniques will be used:

1. We may say, "Sometimes we have difficulty in agreeing with our friends, let alone those with whom we have little in common, but let's be objective, and consider the other viewpoint. It is difficult, I know, but you are a fair-minded person . . ."
2. If you are able to do so when meeting A and B, refer to other similar situations which have been resolved by goodwill on both sides.
3. Always isolate the main differences between the parties. Obtaining agreement on minor differences is not usually difficult, which means that we can then concentrate our efforts on settling the main reason for the conflict.
4. Never allow A and B to state their case while together in your company. Obviously they will have to be brought together, and when that time arrives, we must give our decision. But A and B must not then be given the opportunity to restate their points of view. If this happens, A will interrupt B and B will interrupt A, and the conflict will boil over again.

"We shall attempt to settle on a fifty-fifty basis, with neither side winning or losing. A fifty-fifty compromise may annoy the protagonists initially, but this annoyance will soon be forgotten as each of them explains to his associates the points he has won, while omitting those he has lost.

"My message, therefore, is that for high quality

management there must be management of stress, change, and conflict."

Once more there was applause, and there followed a lengthy discussion.

At 4 pm a steward arrived with tea and cakes.

11 Recruiting high quality people

Brennan began the final session, "The reason why many companies perform so badly, why there is perhaps too much stress and conflict, is because of the old tag: *You can't make a silk purse out of a sow's ear.* If the quality of the staff is poor or at best average, success is almost impossible to attain.

"This may not be due to an incompetent Board. The Board might consist of brilliant engineers, financial geniuses, or strategic wonders, but if no one is able to obtain the best possible teams, whether in the factory, office, or the field, then their brilliance will be of no avail or at best it will make their objectives much harder to achieve. Therefore, to succeed, we must have *high quality typists, high quality packers, high quality supervisors, high quality salesmen.* The cause of much of the failure in so many companies, as I have said, is the employment of less than average men and women, mainly due to an inability to interview and select correctly in the first place."

As Brennan paused, Spurling said, "Then why not employ personnel selection consultants? We've used them in the past."

Wallace thought Brennan's smile was a trifle grim as he continued, "Firstly, there is no guarantee that the person assigned to us by the consultancy group is going to be someone of any great experience. He may have joined the consultancy company two or three weeks earlier. He would have had training, but that is very limited with the smaller consultants. Secondly, the cost is high – possibly 15 or 20 per cent of the first year's salary of the applicant. Do you know what is often the real reason for personnel consultants being employed?"

Several heads were shaken, and Brennan continued, "In this era of insecurity few managers want to be held responsible for mistakes, and this applies especially to the larger companies. In the USA it has reached the position where a manager will call in a consultant if the building needs painting, in case he should get the colour wrong."

"I hardly think that applies in this country," said Spurling.

"It isn't a point worth debating, but I am telling you that it is sometimes a reason for hiring personnel selection consultants. We shall interview and engage our own staff, which, in my opinion, is the right way to build the best possible team. If a manager is given no training whatsoever in interviewing and selection, it might well be better to employ consultants. But there are so many training courses available today that there is really no excuse for a manager not doing the job for which he is employed.

"For 99 per cent of vacancies, consultants can do no better than a manager who has advertised the position in the national or trade press. Does that clear that up?"

Brennan glanced at his companions. No one spoke, so he went on, "We shall devote this session to the art of finding the right square peg for the square hole, and the first vacancy we have to fill is, of course, a quality control manager. What then, Harvey, is the first step in recruitment?"

The response was immediate. "Draw up a job specification, followed by a man specification. Then draw up an advertisement based on these specifications."

"Right!" said Brennan. "And that is exactly what you

are going to do now – though strictly speaking, of course, this should be a man or woman specification."

"Me?"

"No, all of you. I want you to get together as a syndicate and produce these specifications. When they are complete, we shall draw up an advertisement, and discuss the interviewing and selection techniques."

Brennan glanced at his wristwatch. "I shall be back in twenty minutes or so, and that should be long enough for you to knock something together." With that, he stood up and left a slightly bemused management team.

He hurried along the passageway to the stairs leading to his cabin, and when he got there, quickly changed into bathing trunks, slipped on the white towelling robe provided by Cunard, and made his way to the Magradrome Centre on the Lido deck.

The Magradrome covered the swimming pool and relaxing areas during bad weather conditions. When the sun shone the Magradrome was rolled back, to allow for open air sunbathing.

It was a cold and showery day, but Brennan, arriving at the pool, found it surrounded by passengers lounging in well padded deckchairs. They showed only a mild interest in the new arrival. He plunged into the pool, swam up and down some twenty times, got out and towelled down. He was about to make his way back to the cabin when a voice called out, "Hello, Bob." It was Brian Moss, who was sitting with his wife Jill.

Brian, fair-haired, broad-shouldered, his waist only slightly broader than when he had played water polo at championship level, now looked the dynamic entrepreneur he was. He stood up and shook hands.

Brennan bent down to kiss Jill lightly on her cheek. He had always told Vivienne that if he hadn't married her, he would have fallen for 'Gorgeous Jill', as he always called her.

Brennan said, "I didn't contact you because I knew

that you wanted this trip to be a bit of a rest cure after the rush and bustle of your life. You were kind enough to agree to interrupt it, to give us one session. Will you join us for drinks tonight, to meet our team?"

"Thanks Bob, but I'd rather meet them after my lecture, otherwise they may ask too many questions in advance and ruin my script. Is it still Wednesday morning you want me?"

"Yes, and we're all looking forward to it. Then we can have a special party for you on Thursday evening. How about that?"

"That'll be fine!"

Brennan said, "I must hurry along now, I'm playing truant."

They laughed, and Brennan moved on. About ten minutes later he returned to the meeting room. The managers all looked rather pleased with themselves.

Wallace was spokesman. "We've produced a job and a man specification," he said. "Here they are for you to consider."

Brennan accepted the sheets of paper, which comprised the following:

JOB SPECIFICATION

Duties
To develop, introduce, and maintain a quality assurance system compliant with BS5750 Part I, so that the company can achieve and retain Approved Capability status granted by the British Standards Institution.

To liaise with BSI and other approval bodies on matters pertaining to quality, and to represent the company's interest in the formulation of approval bodies', industry associations', and customers' quality assurance policies.

To highlight all customers' quality requirements at an

early stage, bring these to the attention of the relevant personnel, and ensure that action is taken to meet these requirements.

To negotiate with customers on all matters concerning quality.

To prepare quality and inspection plans, as required.

To maintain close contact with the other members of the management team on quality matters, and influence departments so that quality is maintained or improved.

To make inputs to design and production engineering identifying potential quality problems at this stage, so that early corrective action can be taken.

To manage inspection activities and personnel, to ensure inspections are performed in a satisfactory and economic manner.

To devise and maintain a fault reporting system, to allow analysis of both product and system faults, to identify problems at an early stage, and initiate corrective action.

To ensure that all personnel are made aware of their role in achieving the company's quality assurance, and provide or organise suitable training as necessary.

To keep abreast of developments in quality assurance and inspection technology, and introduce these into the company where appropriate.

To prepare reports for the board on quality matters, and advise them as requested.

To control quality circles.

To perform other tasks pertinent to quality assurance, as directed by the managing director.

MAN SPECIFICATION

Education and Qualification
Educated to at least HNC level in a relevant engineering discipline.

A member of the Institute of Quality Assurance or other appropriate professional institute.

Some formal training in quality assurance, e.g. external or in-house courses.

Experience

At least three years in a senior position responsible for management of part or all of a quality assurance system in a company with a similar product line.

Proven ability as a man-manager in a unionised environment.

'Hands on' experience handling of measuring tools/equipment.

Experience in the application of statistical analysis and planning techniques.

Knowledgeable and up-to-date with the production processes used in the factory.

To have experience of computers used in design, production, and business control.

Appreciation of business economics and financial controls.

Sound knowledge of appropriate measuring techniques.

Ability to interpret computerised data for analysis and continual improvement of product quality.

Personal

Aged 30-55 years, with a stable background. Acceptable appearance and manner for dealing with customers.

Must have the ability to identify opportunities and potential problems, and have the courage and tenacity to see through the required changes.

Enthusiastic about quality assurance.

Must have the personality and approach to 'fit into' the existing management team.

Able to write concise, accurate reports, and present logical and persuasive arguments, written or oral.

A good man-manager.

Able to deal with both customers and suppliers at all levels.

Capable of training personnel in their quality assurance role.

Ability to say "no" to important customers or suppliers without upsetting them.

Ability to provide useful input to product design/ modification.

When he had finished reading, Brennan said, "Very good. I can see I've already built a magnificent team."

Everyone laughed dutifully.

He went on, "The next step is to draw up an advertisement and decide on the media and space requirements. Before we consider the copy, we shall have to decide on a caption."

Spurling said, "Surely it need only be *Quality Assurance Manager required*. We don't want to interest anyone other than those of experience, do we?"

"Maybe," said Brennan. "Anyone want to add to that?"

Wallace said, "A salary, to attract attention?"

"That can be a two-edged sword," said Brennan. "Someone earning £X might not reply to our offer of £X + 3000, thinking the job out of reach, when it need not necessarily be so. A person earning more than £X + 3000 might decide not to apply, yet he could be the ideal man for the job on offer, and if we interviewed him, we could perhaps negotiate a better salary package. What do you think we should do? State a salary in spite of my reservations?"

They all thought it might still be advisable to state the salary, but Brennan still demurred. "Wouldn't we," he said, "get the best of all worlds if we used some ambiguous phrase – for example, *Remuneration package in keeping with the importance of the position?*"

"I don't like that kind of vague statement," said

Spurling. "To me it would convey the impression that the advertiser first wanted to find out what the applicant was earning and then offer as little more as he thinks he could get away with. Maybe someone would agree to a salary several thousand pounds below what the advertisers might be prepared to pay."

"And is there anything wrong with that?" asked Brennan.

"Yes," said Spurling, "it's unethical."

"Why? If the applicant is getting the job which satisfies him and the advertiser is also satisfied, I can't see anything wrong with it. In addition, it gives the advertiser the opportunity of motivating the applicant if he does well, by giving him a salary increase much sooner than would normally be usual."

There followed a general discussion, and eventually they all agreed, though some reluctantly, that the open-ended remuneration package might be the right way to influence a candidate.

Brennan said, "It could mean we pay more, it could mean we pay less. I'm prepared to pay whatever a person is worth, and the higher the pay the better I shall like it . . ."

Spurling interrupted him. "In view of what you have just said I believe you should offer a very high salary for a quality assurance manager."

"And I agree," said Brennan, "but do Mike's views change the decision? Let's vote on it. To state a high salary in an advertisement or an open-ended remuneration package?"

It was generally agreed that when a high salary was being offered, it should be advertised.

Brennan then switched back to the caption. He said, "The heading, then, will be *Quality Assurance Manager* plus salary. Now, is that right or wrong?"

"Wrong!" said Harvey Strong. "We don't have to include the word *Assurance* – *Quality Manager* will do.

There's no need to add unnecessary words in an advertisement."

"I agree," said Brennan. "So the heading will be *Quality Manager* plus salary. Is that enough to attract the attention of the ideal candidate?"

"No," said Strong once more. "I've been checking, and there are often several advertisements for quality managers with which we shall have to compete. We have to have a special appeal if we are to attract the attention of the ideal candidate."

Wallace said, "But won't the salary win the day and knock out competition?"

"Not necessarily," said Strong. "We're not looking for the *has-beens* or the *never-wasers*. We don't want the butterflies who flit from job to job. We don't want the failures who know it's the end of the line for them so they begin studying the ads. We want the highly successful quality manager who is considering changing his job, but will only do so if an offer is attractive enough. Remember, no employee is ever wholly satisfied with his boss or his income."

Brennan smiled brightly, but said nothing.

Strong continued, "We have to be different. We have to attract the attention not of the regular studier of advertisements but of the glancer, who might just be persuaded to change his job if the offer is attractive enough."

"Well let's have your ideas," said Brennan. "I know you've worked it all out."

"Too true! Over and over again one or the other of us has emphasised that if you, Bob, were not deeply concerned with quality the scheme would be a flop. Wouldn't you say that one of the main reasons why a quality manager might want to change his job is because he is not happy about the backing given to him by top management? May I suggest a caption?"

"Go ahead," said Brennan.

"How about the following?

OUR QUALITY-MINDED MANAGING DIRECTOR WILL GIVE ONE HUNDRED PER CENT BACKING TO AN OUTSTANDING QUALITY MANAGER

"Then the copy can read:

And management team backs the managing director in his decision to maintain and improve the quality of our products.

"Then can follow all the benefits of joining our company, and extracts from the job description and man specification. And only then," went on Strong, "shall we use the clincher, i.e. the top salary we are offering – this to obtain some immediate action on the part of the reader of the advertisement."

Strong got a handclap for his creativity, and Brennan said, "How long did it take you to think up that excellent caption?"

Strong grinned. "Since you told me that at the meeting interviewing and selection would be included, some time ago."

Brennan said, "And therein lies a lesson for us all. Most advertisements for staff are dreadfully unimaginative, boring to read, cliché-ridden, and based mostly on the *I-we-you* formula, which means that the advertising copy is all about what the advertising wants and very little about what the applicant is looking for. That formula should always be *You-we-I*.

"It takes a lot of thinking to draft an advertisement – thinking while you are driving the car, thinking while you are at home . . . But the formula, one of the oldest in the selling world, is as applicable to advertising as it is to selling:

"Attract attention.

"Arouse interest.

"Create the desire to reply to the advertisement.

"And then – an action close.

"Our advertisement must, in the main, stress the benefits to the applicant if he joins the company. Too many advertisers think they are doing someone a favour by offering them a job. This may well be the case, but it doesn't apply to the ideal applicant.

"He does the company a favour by joining it. All too many companies settle for second best because their aim is for second best. Our aim is for quality, and we want the best quality manager available."

The discussion continued for some time. Then Brennan said, "Now for the next point. Do we ask for a full *Curriculum Vitae* or do we invite candidates to write in for an application form? Your views, please."

Wallace answered, "An application form, every time. It sets out clearly all the information required, and as questions have to be answered, it may include information which would not otherwise be given in a written CV. It means also that all the applicants are being assessed by the same standards."

Brennan nodded, but made no comment.

Then Hemmings took up the issue. "I agree with Laurie, if only because so many applicants write almost illegibly, but when asked to complete an application form they usually think more carefully, write more slowly, and their writing is, therefore, legible."

"A fair comment," said Brennan. "How about you, Mike?"

Spurling said, "I'm open-minded. Most shop floor workers don't fill in application forms anyway, although the standard employment forms are completed."

Strong said briefly, "I believe application forms are a waste of time. I prefer to invite applicants to telephone me. I know the right questions to ask to bring the answers I want."

Clayton said, "I, too, think application forms are time-wasting. They don't apply to service engineers, and I don't think they apply either to a management position. Such applicants usually send in a very full CV, and to ask them to duplicate it on an application form serves no purpose."

Brennan said, "Thank you, gentlemen. My own view is that application forms in the main have outlived their usefulness. At one time I was a most fervent advocate of their use. I believed they helped to clarify one's mind and led to a logical step by step interview. Nowadays that no longer applies. Any worthwhile applicant would devise a CV that not only showed him in a good light but gave all the facts that a prospective employer needed to decide whether an interview was worth while.

"The applicant who doesn't send in a well set out CV is rarely worth interviewing anyway. Any candidate of ability will add to his CV details which are relevant to the position advertised, showing that he has read the advertisement carefully.

"And finally, when seeking the ideal applicant, there is always a time risk. For example, the quality manager we want may be in touch with another company and may have to decide between us. Will he delay a decision for a week or so while he writes a letter asking for an application form, completes the form on its arrival, posts it back and then awaits a response?

"My view is that only in exceptional circumstances are application forms needed. A request in an advertisement for a full CV is enough. Those in favour?"

"Is that a request or a demand?" asked Hemmings with a laugh.

"A request, of course!"

After further discussion they all agreed that only a CV was required.

Brennan continued, "So we have the job specification and the man specification from which we have devised the advertisement. We have the appealing caption, and the copy with the strong salary appeal close.

"But before we continue, you mentioned inviting telephone calls, Harvey. What do the others think about that?"

"It doesn't work," said Laurie Wallace, "unless the request to telephone is only for an application form, in which case anyone can take the call. If it is to telephone a specific person – say you, Mike – the chances are that you'll not be available when the calls come in. If the calls are taken by a secretary or a receptionist, they will not be able to deal adequately with the callers' questions. They can only ask him to ring back or ask for his telephone number.

"Sometimes they will take it upon themselves to ask questions or give information, and that can so easily put off the ideal applicant. Communication by telephone is an art acquired by few people."

"I've used it successfully many times," said Strong.

"Of course," answered Wallace, "because you advertise for salesmen. The same might apply if you were advertising for various types of office staff, but it doesn't apply to a management position. The reason for this is that when you advertise for a salesman, you make sure that you are available to receive the calls, and you do know how to handle them; so do your area managers.

"Furthermore, salesmen are never expected to sit down and write CVs – they prefer to telephone.

"Another weakness is that if the advertisement is a good one, the telephone lines can get jammed. This has happened to you, Harvey, as I well know. It could mean that the ideal applicant gets tired of ringing and doesn't try again."

A slightly mollified Strong sat back in his chair, stroking his beard. He said, "Well, may I make another plea about the use of the telephone?"

"No," said Brennan. "We've covered that ground pretty well."

"But I'm referring to it in a different context."

Brennan shrugged his shoulders. "OK, Harvey, you can't win against a salesman! Go ahead."

"A CV doesn't reflect an applicant's manner, the quality of his thinking or his personality. This means that possibly 50 per cent of the applicants are granted an interview, only for the interviewer to discover very quickly that good though his CV may have been, the applicant doesn't match up to it, for a variety of reasons. Once the interiew has been granted, however, out of courtesy the interviewer has to go through some of the standard procedures. When I use a CV for regional managers, for example, I never invite applicants to attend an interview without first speaking to them over the telephone."

Again Strong stroked his beard, a habit which was irritating both Hemmings and Wallace.

"Are you saying," asked Spurling, "that you can form a judgement over the telephone?"

"Most certainly! We're always judging people over the telephone. We're put off by the dreariness of a voice or the sharpness of its tone, by an uninspired manner or a dictatorial manner, a lack of quality in thinking – almost a lack of interest in the job offered. It all comes out over the telephone if the right questions are asked. You can very quickly tell the applicant who really wants a particular job from the applicant who believes he can tackle any job and writes to a wide variety of advertisers. But if any doubts remain, I always give them the benefit, and arrange an interview."

There were differing views on Strong's techniques, but once more they all agreed that this was a simple and effective way of saving the time of both applicants and manager.

Then Brennan said, "Now for quality interviewing techniques, which will be followed by what in my opinion is the 99 per cent certain way of choosing the right applicant if he is available.

"You all know about structured interviewing, or interviews based on a six-or eight-point plan. All good systems, but usually quite unnecesary. There are only three main qualities that you want to discover in the applicant at an interview. Any ideas on that subject?"

Wallace said, "Ability, skills, application."

Hemmings said, "Integrity, aptitude, substantiation of evidence."

Clayton said, "Manner, qualifications, willingness to co-operate."

Spurling said, "For me it's mostly technical skills, attitude, and are they militants or not?"

Brennan said, "That's a good selection, and you're all right. But they are all covered by my three points.

"First, we want to know whether we can work with the applicant. There's so much nonsense written about the halo effect, which means we are motivated to engage someone who wears the old school tie, has a similar background, enjoys the same hobbies, and we are told that we should ignore these halo effects. Why? If we work well with people, the chances are that we shall benefit both the company and ourselves, provided, naturally, that they have the essential qualities of skill to line up with the job specification.

"The second essential is to discover the validity of all the claims made in the applicant's CV.

"And the third step is to ensure that in all respects the candidate measures up to our man specification."

There was some discussion, then, "Let us first concentrate on the pitfalls of interviewing which may mislead us or cloud our judgement."

Wallace said, "I'd like to raise another point first, Bob."

"Carry on."

"You talked about discovering whether you or others could work with an applicant. That means you are assessing someone. How can the inexperienced interviewer make such an assessment? I know you can, I believe I could, but there are others besides us who engage staff."

"That's a good question, Laurie. But how does the professional interviewer make his assessment? By visual judgement, by listening carefully and by considering the CV. Anyone can take those three steps."

Wallace shrugged his shoulders. "Do you mean to say, Bob, that one of our area service managers who had to take on service engineers could make such assessments?"

"Most decidedly! They, and we, are assessing people all the time. We're right probably 85 per cent of the time, and women are usually right in their judgements over 90 per cent of the time. Professional interviewers won't do much better than that!

"When we meet someone, whether for a few minutes' chat or for a longer conversation, we assess them very quickly, and we see through them pretty speedily as well. We label them boasters, compulsive talkers, bores, miseries, phoneys. I should think every one of our wives, at some time or another, has said about someone, 'I don't trust him', and she's nearly always right.

"We all have this animal instinct. An animal judges very quickly whether someone is a friend or foe, and we have the same attributes.

"Laurie, I assure you, our judgements are nearly always right, as those of your area managers will be if they interview. Remember, I'm talking about people who have already achieved some form of management level."

Clayton said, "But how about con men – those who put on an act that we can't see through? People are being conned all the time."

"True," said Brennan, "but luckily they are only a tiny minority, and I'll tell you later how to discover whether an applicant is lying or not. Forget your doubts. I assure you that the experience of many of us has proved this to be right.

"Now let me run through the brief rules we have discussed so far:

1. We can only find the candidate to meet our needs if we provide a job and man specification.
2. Draw up an advertisement which will appeal to the ideal applicant.
3. Remember that to win over the ideal applicant will need persuasiveness on our part. We have to resolve not to let the ideal candidate get away to take a position elsewhere.
4. In the advertisement we ask for a full CV and work from that.
5. We turn down all applicants who do not meet our man specification. If we don't do this, there is no sense in having such a standard. For example, if we require an HNC or relevant standard, it is no use accepting someone who may appeal to us but perhaps has only managed to get half way through the course. The applicant will, of course, insist that his experience is all we require. If that argument is acceptable, it will apply to the full man specification; if, for example, the age group requirement is between thirty and forty-five, we might have to consider accepting forty-six. But if that is acceptable, why not forty-seven, forty-eight, and so on? Then why have a man specification at all?
6. The first assessment is on the applicant's CV, the second assessment by talking to the applicant over the telephone.
7. We have three objectives at the interview: to assess the likelihood of the applicant working well with us

and our associates; to make certain the claims he makes for his aptitudes, experience, and technical skills are true; to make certain that we are not being used as a stopgap.

8. Interviewing techniques are extremely simple, but we do need constant reminders of their simplicity. For example, we must set out to relax the applicant by using the opening gambit of asking some simple questions. How long have you lived in your house? Does your wife work? I see you have a son of thirteen, how is he getting on at school? Only a few minutes are needed to ask questions, which will put the applicant at ease. These are then followed by a host of open questions:

Tell me more about why you left your two previous positions.
Why do you think you would have a good future with our company?
Explain a little more about the work you are doing.

"These questions, of course, are all based on the statements made in his CV.

9. Look out for any signs of a cover-up. Here are some typical ones, which arouse suspicion. First, 'I've been working abroad for the last two years.' That's fair enough if the employer is a well known company. It is not so OK if the applicant claims he was working for himself, or that the company he was working for has gone into liquidation.

   Another point often used as a cover-up is when exact dates have not been given by the applicant of when he joined a company and when he left. There is, possibly, a gap that the applicant wishes to hide. The question must be put to him: *What did you do during this time?*

   The claim that an applicant was working on his own might be quite genuine, but it could also be suspect, especially if the claim is made over a long period of time.

Past employers are apt to forget, or prepared to overlook, misdemeanours on the part of the applicant when there has been a long time gap. In addition, the applicant's immediate past chief may no longer be with the company. When this happens, a standard reference is given, and that can mean very little.

One explanation, which is given continually and is always suspect, is *I left for personal reasons.* The point to discover then is who did the applicant quarrel with, and why? In such instances we often hear, *The manager was impossible to work with. Nobody can work with him.* But people rarely leave for such personal reasons unless they already have another, better job lined up.

If there is a gap after leaving a company for personal reasons, then we should be more suspicious than ever.

"Now we must reverse the procedure, and think of the way the candidate is summing us up. He knows that we may be suspect in several directions. Candidates are used to being interviewed, and they know that most interviewers exaggerate the benefits of the position on offer and play down the problems. If the applicant suspects that we are not telling the truth, he may not want to accept the position. If he should accept the position, there could be problems after he has started work – he could feel let down.

"At the interview we must be truthful. We must tell the applicant exactly what the position entails. We must dash any hopes of immediate promotion, which some interviewers offer as a carrot to persuade an applicant to join the company. We must give the true reason why a previous employee may have left, and the reason for the vacancy.

"We will, of course, stress truthful benefits all the time, but if there are warts, we must explain these, and leave the applicant to judge whether they are acceptable. That is the way to obtain ideal people, and more important, to retain them.

"These are just a few of the pitfalls of which we must be aware. Can anyone think of others?"

Wallace, who was not impressed by the pitfalls emphasised by Brennan, because he felt that all managers worthy of the name must already be aware of them, was about to point this out when Spurling said, "Do you know, Bob, I've been a manager for many years and I've done my share of interviewing and engaging staff. I can see now that I was only about 50 per cent effective. My advertisements were wrong. I interviewed in the belief that I was doing them a favour by inviting them to join us, and I certainly wasn't aware of many of the pitfalls you've just mentioned. I've been apt to take people at their face value and believe what they've told me."

Hemmings chuckled. "Mike," he said, "you'll never be a managing director if you think like that! Eh, Bob?"

Brennan said, "That's not fair! Mike is only admitting that he is a wiser man today than he was yesterday. But you're right, managing directors do become a little cynical. You must remember that most people do tell the truth, are honest, and decent. We all make excuses for ourselves when we bend the rules a little, but that's all some applicants are doing when they try to mislead the interviewer. So you see, although a managing director may become cynical, if in doubt, he must be prepared to believe in the loyalty, decency, and honesty of an associate or an applicant who is applying for a position.

"The oft quoted tag *Let the buyer beware* does apply to interviewing and selection. *Let the interviewer beware* is also a reasonable dictum. But that doesn't mean that an applicant who maybe runs off with his best friend's wife may not be the ideal candidate for a specific job, only that the interviewer should be aware of all the facts and then take the *bad* from the *good*. If the balance is still with the *good*, the applicant may still be the ideal person for the job."

Wallace was glad Spurling had spoken before him, and saved him from indirectly criticising Brennan, when, obviously, all the managers knew little about interviewing techniques.

There was some further discussion and then Brennan said, "Now for the 99 per cent certain method of making the right decision: References must be taken up, and this applies just as much to a shorthand-typist as to any executive. But they shouldn't be taken up in the usual way. Written references are almost always useless. These days there are too many legal implications if the truth were told about a past employee who may have been dismissed. Personnel managers are reluctant to put into writing their true reasons for the dismissal, or to give the facts about the weaknesses of one of their past employees. I know of a case where the man was given a reasonable reference although he had been dismissed for hitting a supervisor. The police had not been called in and he had not been charged with any offence. Therefore, he claimed, if his employers gave him a bad reference, he would take them to court; so they gave him a misleading reference. They didn't say anything good about the man, but they didn't say anything bad, either.

"If a check were made, I think you would find that some 70 per cent of interviewers don't take up references at all. Possibly some 29 per cent make a written request, which, as I have said, is almost valueless. The remaining 1 per cent is made up of enlightened managers who know how to elicit the truth.

"You may ask how do I arrive at these figures. Well, of course, they are guestimates, but the fact is that over many years as a manager I have lost staff, some for the right reasons, some because they have been dismissed. The number of times I have been asked for a reference has been infinitesimal. I think, therefore, I may have erred on the generous side, statistically.

"But if you're looking for quality staff, you have to take trouble to make sure that you never employ anybody who cannot play his part in the growth of the company, and may even have an adverse effect on others. What I have always done is to telephone past employers."

Hemmings said, "But would a past employer speak freely over the telephone?"

"Always, if the correct technique is used. The risk of not taking up references is so great. Let me give you an example. A well known hotel group wanted a managing director to take control of one of its hotels. An applicant applied, and references of the standard variety were taken up.

"It soon became apparent that the applicant was an alcoholic, although no mention was made of that in the letters from past employers. The hotel had to pay quite heavily to get rid of the man and then, believe it or not, he got another very good job with another hotel where, again, they had written the usual request for a reference, and received the usual reply. Finally, very rarely will anybody write in a letter of reference that a person is a trouble-maker. Have I made my case?"

"Yes," said Hemmings, "but surely you can't telephone a candidate's employer while he is still working for that company."

"Let me explain. When interviewing, three decisions have to be made: one, those not suitable are turned down; two, if the choice is between several applicants, possibly the decision may have to be postponed; and three, you believe you have found the ideal candidate and want to offer him the job.

"When interviewing the several possibles, or the ideal person, you will obviously ask each of them to whom you may apply for a reference. You will confirm immediately that no references will be taken up until the applicant has decided to join the company. This agreed, you will continue, 'The first decision is yours. I have given you all the facts. If we talked for another week, there would be no further information I could give you; therefore, if I offered you the job now, would you accept?'

"If the candidate wants to think things over, you have not been convincing enough or else he is considering another offer. This lack of enthusiasm on the applicant's part would, except under exceptional circumstances, rule him out. The excuse *I want to think things over* is not valid; it doesn't denote a person of great depth of thought. The candidate applied for the position. If he didn't want to make a change, he shouldn't have applied. If he is uncertain of your job offer, this is not the attitude you want. Why engage someone so reluctant to join you? Anyway, you will find most such applicants subsequently refuse the offer, and the minority are not worth engaging.

"There are always exceptions to this rule, especially at managing director level, but they are few in number.

"Now let us assume that those short-listed or the one ideal all agree to accept the offer, if it is made to them. You will explain your reason for telephoning for references. You will emphasise that you will not, however, telephone until you have made the decision to engage him, subject to references, and he has informed his company.

"You might say something like, 'I'll probably ask what is wrong with you – by the way, how do you think your chief would answer that question?' It's surprising how illuminating the replies can be. The applicant will do one of three things: He will answer, 'I don't think he will disagree with anything I have told you about myself.' If he has had problems with his company, he may use this as a bluff, hoping that the truth will not emerge. This is standard practice when an employee is under notice or has just left a company.

"Alternatively, he is telling the truth, and knows that his employer will speak well of him. Or, again, he knows that the telephone call will find him out. He will pretend all is well, but he will telephone later to tell you that he has decided not to accept your job as he has had a better offer.

"The same may apply even to the ideal candidate. We can all misjudge people, but my system means that we learn the truth, every time.

"Is the procedure clear now, Richard?"

"Yes, it is."

"Good. Then let us go on to consider how we can be sure of learning the truth from the ex-employer. Let us assume that I am telephoning a Mr Brown. When I have explained the reason for my call in the past, the "Mr Browns" have never refused to speak to me. My opening words are, 'My name is Brennan of Linklaters, you may have heard of us.' If he hasn't, a short explanation may be necessary to prove that my company is a company of some standing. Then, 'John X has applied to us for the position of transport manager. I'm sure you will agree that written references don't help a lot, Mr Brown, and that's why I am telephoning you to ask your opinion.' Pause there, then say, 'Mr Brown, would you prefer to telephone me back, to check my bona fides?' Sometimes this offer is taken up, but it is surprising how rarely.

"You will, first, check on technical qualifications, skills, and experience. Then, after you are sure that the applicant is well worth engaging in these respects, you can make use of either of two techniques for eliciting the truth.

"You will, then, continue, 'John X has a good record, although he has changed his job quite a few times. But I have been interviewing for many years, and somehow I sense something is wrong – there is a missing link.' "

Brennan paused. Then he said to his managers, "*There is a missing link* is the key phrase. Remember that. Now I will go back to my talk with Mr Brown: 'I'm sure you know what that is, Mr Brown. Can you tell me in confidence? It may not affect the job offer, but it may be to John X's advantage, as well as ours, if we know of his weaknesses as well as his strengths.'

"I assure you that the question, put that way, will nine times out of ten result in the 'Mr Browns' of the world saying, 'He is a very good man but . . .' and then will come the explanation: 'he's difficult to get on with,' 'he had rather a lot of illness,' 'he has problems at home,' and so on.

"Alternatively, instead of using the 'link' technique, you can use the 'assumption' technique, saying something like, 'Mr Brown, John X has rather a lazy look about him,' 'He doesn't seem very ambitious,' 'He seems the type of man who talks rather than acts,' or 'I have the feeling that he may drink a little too much.'

"Again, by making these assumptions, you may discover the truth. Remember no applicant is 100 per cent perfect, and we are trying to discover his serious weaknesses. Most ordinary weaknesses are acceptable, if the applicant measures up to the man specification.

"Sometimes when you ask Mr Brown's advice, he will answer, 'I'd rather not discuss that, you'll have to find out for yourself.' On these occasions, whatever you do, never engage that applicant.

"Finally, if in doubt, ask the question, 'If you had a vacancy, Mr Brown, would you re-engage John X?' If, then, there is a pause and Mr Brown begins with, 'Well – er . . .' followed by another pause, or by some joking remark, such as 'I must have notice of that question!,' again don't engage John X.

"Gentlemen, these procedures for ensuring that you only engage high quality people will never let you down. There is no other way of discovering the truth about an applicant, whether it be his techinical skills, his creativity, or his ability to get along with other people.

"Psychologists, behavioural scientists, graphologists, will never find out so much about an applicant as you can by telephoning his past employer.

"There is only one way of engaging staff, and that is to work on the lines I have indicated. Past employers, like a man's family, do know the truth about him, his weaknesses and his strengths. Again, I confirm that if all the right techniques are used, you will be 99 per cent correct every time.

"Once more I ask you, have I made my case?"

The applause with which he was greeted indicated that he had won them over.

"That's fine," he said, "and there is one final point. You may spend a thousand pounds or more on advertising a vacancy, but *never* engage anyone who is second best. I am referring to the applicant who stands out because the others interviewed are well below average. You are being unfair to the applicant, as well as to yourself, when you engage such a person. So scrap the campaign and start all over again."

Brennan glanced at his watch. "We have a few more minutes," he said. "Harvey you've probably interviewed many more people than any of us. I'm sure I've missed out several points. Would you like to add your views?"

"You've covered it all very well, Bob, but there are three or four more points if you would like to hear them.

1. Avoid making notes during an interview. Surely it isn't asking a lot of an interviewer to expect him to remember all the details during the thirty-or forty-minute period. Notes can be made subsequently. But it's very off-putting to an applicant to see an interviewer jotting down notes on a piece of paper.
2. Never ask nonsensical questions such as *Are you a self-starter? Are you a hard worker? Are you ambitious?* All applicants answer these questions correctly, and they serve no purpose.

3. You can judge an applicant by the kind of questions he asks you – are they sensible, or not? I always allow my applicants to ask me a lot of questions – in fact, I invite them to do so.

"That's about all – oh yes, one final point: I never never allow a good applicant to get away. I believe it to be a selling job on my part to persuade him to join my company. I don't allow ideal applicants to go away to think things over; there may be too many companies competing for them."

He was about to go on, but paused. "I'm getting black looks from Laurie and glares from Richard. I think they're all getting a bit thirsty."

"Aren't we all!" said Brennan. "But there are still one or two points for discussion . . ."

At six pm the meeting ended. It had been a long, hard day and there was little time to shower, shave, and change into dinner jacket before attending the captain's welcoming cocktail party.

Later that evening one of the managers telephoned Mark Cornell, managing director of Canada Copiers, at his home address.

12   All at sea

It was seven am on the second full day at sea. Mary Clayton had decided to breakfast in bed, while her husband met colleagues for breakfast at eight am.

The sea had developed a low swell, which, allied to a strong wind, aroused some unease amongst the first-timers, although it had little effect on the hardened passengers.

The sea didn't worry the Claytons. Mary was happy and content, enjoying every minute of her rare break from domestic chores. Before leaving for breakfast Victor said, "I'm keeping my options open. The question I can't make up my mind about is whether or not Brennan is too good to be true."

"I like him," said Mary, simply.

Harvey Strong swallowed two anti-seasick pills and said, "God, it's rough!"

Pat said, "It isn't really, darling. It's all in your imagination."

"Don't talk bloody nonsense, it's rough! I don't know how I shall be able to sit through this morning's session. What'll I do if I'm seasick during the session?"

"Run out to the nearest loo."

"I don't know where that is, and I don't want to make a bloody fool of myself in front of the others."

He sat for a few moments, contemplating his un-happiness before taking a deep breath and saying, "What are you going to do this morning, Pat?"

"I'm listening to a talk by a Steiner manager on *How to become more glamorous*. Tina's coming with me. She's a poppet, so clever, too." Then her tone changed. "Do you think everything is going well?"

"Sure! But I'm not worried. I can look after myself."

At seven-thirty Richard and Penny Hemmings were jogging around the deck, both dressed for the occasion in blue outfits. Pausing for a few moments to watch the ship's wake, Penny said, "She's so bossy, that's her trouble!"

"Who is?"

"I told you a few moments ago, that Wallace woman. She's always so adamant about everything."

"And is that bad?"

"It is when she argues about everything. If I get through this voyage without telling her what I think of her it will be a miracle!"

Laurie Wallace had a splitting headache. His unsympathetic wife told him it served him right, he should have cut down on his drinking on the first night out. Wallace didn't reply, but moved another notch in the belt around his trouser waist, tightening it as much as he could in the hope of disguising the overhanging bulge.

Dorothy said, "Do you believe he will make you a director?"

"Yes, I do," Wallace answered. "I do indeed! But if not, I have my alternatives."

Tina Spurling was reading the ship's newspaper, which, as usual, contained very little news.

"The strike's still on," she said.

"There's always some strike on!"

"But it doesn't seem so bad when there are only two lines about it, instead of pages."

"I must hurry," said Mike.

"Why?"

"Because I don't want to be late, and I'm hungry."

"You're always hungry. But I'm still worried about our future. This seems such an unnecessary expense."

Spurling shook his head. "It's the best investment Bob's made. He's probing us, watching our every move, summing us up."

"Do you like him?"

"Like doesn't enter into it. No top man is ever liked all the time. He gives, and he is liked; he refuses, and he's disliked. I'm keeping my options open."

13 Quality control

When Brennan entered the meeting room at nine am, the managers were awaiting him. After the usual greetings Brennan said, "Today, the accent will be on *Quality in Production*. This may mean that some of you will switch off. Later, when Harvey talks to us about *Quality in Salesmanship*, others will switch off.

"This lack of concentration is due to the belief that production is solely the affair of the engineers, while selling is for salesmen. If you do concentrate, however, you will find that the quality lessons in both these subjects apply to all of us. When we talk about getting the specification of a product right, this can also apply to the design of an office, the production of a leaflet, or the purchase of a desk. But most important is my belief that to be a specialist manager is not enough. We must be all-rounders if we are to succeed – and succeed quickly."

He paused, then continued, "To start us off on the right quality lines we have as our guest speaker, as you know, Brian Moss." Brennan glanced at his watch. "He should be arriving about now. I'll go out and meet him."

With that, Brennan left the managers waiting expectantly for the arrival of 'Mr Quality' himself.

On his return Brennan said, "Let me introduce Brian, who has so kindly agreed to come along and give up some of his 'recuperation' time. His wife tells me he is a seven-day-a-week man so far as work is concerned, and it took her a long time to persuade him to relax for some five days at sea.

"Brian, besides being managing director of NuAire, one of the largest and most successful companies of its kind, is also on the board of several other companies. During his years in office as president of the Heating, Ventilating and Air Conditioning Manufacturers' Association he was largely instrumental in bringing Quality Standards to the ventilating industry.

"He is now chairman of the advisory group on standards for the economic development committee for building, and he is the driving force behind *certification of air moving equipment*, a quality assurance scheme run by the British Standards Institution.

"He is in constant demand as a speaker on Quality Assurance. Gentlemen – Brian Moss."

Moss acknowledged the applause with a "Thank you", and remained standing when Brennan sat down. He began, "Gentlemen, in everyday speech, quality is synonymous with excellence. However, this definition cannot satisfy an engineer brought up on a fare of measurement and analysis. The quality of any thing, product or service, can be classed as both good or bad, depending on what is required of it. Good quality as far as one application is concerned may be bad quality for another. For instance, a cooking utensil that may be perfectly suited to a domestic kitchen is likely to be considered poor quality by a chef working in a busy commercial restaurant. The chef's utensil, however, is not substantial enough to cope with the rough treatment handed out to equipment in a field kitchen, and would be rejected by an army cook as of poor quality.

"Because industry, generally, defines what is required in terms of a specification, the definition is often manipulated into *good quality is meeting the specification.*

"Returning to our ubiquitous kitchen utensil, the quality of the three products required to work in domestic, commercial, and military kitchens depends on them satisfying quite different specifications, even though the function and form of the utensil are identical in each of the applications. This example illustrates the danger inherent in the definition that *good quality is meeting the specification*. What if the terms of the specification do not accurately reflect the true needs of the customer? There may be dissatisfaction when a specification is not met, but it is as nothing compared to the unhappiness over total compliance with a poor specification. Then more than one party is aggrieved, and what begins as a seemingly straightforward quality dispute quickly degenerates into an argument about responsibilities and apportionment of blame.

"There is a story told in the engineering industry which I should like to believe is apocryphal but which experience tells me is probably absolutely true. A well known company contracted out a job for what was intended to be a fairly crude jig. Unfortunately the drawings were prepared on the company's headed tracing sheets, which bore standard tolerance allowances appropriate to their famous very high precision products. It wasn't at all easy for the jig manufacturers to fabricate the jig to these demanding tolerances, but it was probably less easy for the company engineers to swallow the price, and their pride when they discovered what had happened.

"The cynical may well comment, 'But the jig was of good quality. It not only met the specification but, undoubtedly, in this case, performed its intended purpose.'

"My own opinion is that in this case *quality* was not interpreted correctly. *Just right* is good quality. *Slackness* on either side represents poor quality. The great advantage of this interpretation is that it lays the *cost* bogey. Using the definition *good quality is exact fitness for intended purpose* leads us naturally and, in my view, correctly to regard excessive cost as the result of poor quality; unnecessary cost can always be attributed either to over-specifying or to exceeding the demands of the specification.

"My interpretation totally invalidates the objections of those whose philosophy is encapsulated in the wonderfully revealing question they often pose, *Can we afford quality?* I'm not sure, if I were employed by Marks & Spencer, or the Germans or Japanese, whether this attitude would make me squirm or celebrate!

"A book analysing the common qualities exhibited by America's thirty most successful companies concludes that all of them are *obsessed* – author's word, not mine – with *quality*. The list of outstanding *quality-based* companies says it all. These successful firms, far from losing money, save money by good quality. And no wonder! Recently I read that we spend about 30 per cent of our time correcting errors – ours and others'. I can't be sure about the accuracy of the percentage, but I am confident that none of you would argue with the point the author was making. The British Standards Institution has captured the essence of the message in its slogan *Get it right first time*.

"If only we, at NuAire, had known more about quality years ago we'd have saved many, many thousands of pounds, and I would have been saved many, many sleepless nights! Let me tell you the sad story.

"In the earliest days of NuAire we had a problem which severely affected our performance at the time, and would probably have caused an unsupported firm to collapse. Looking back in the dispassionate manner that time allows, the problem was one of poor quality.

"We had started manufacturing a unique product – a small fan unit that could extract air from an internal bathroom or WC through long lengths of four inch diameter piping. The design of the unit coincided with a boom in the building of domestic dwellings, and sales rocketed.

"To satisfy the various bye-laws and building regulations, the units incorporated a timing device which extended the operation of the fan some twenty minutes after the room light switch was turned off. This run-on guaranteed that the area was thoroughly ventilated after occupation. The timer was built around a geared motor. It was simple, reliable, and robust, but it suffered from a major disadvantage. It could not re-cock itself if the light switch was turned on during the timing cycle; therefore, we could not claim that there would always be a twenty minute purging period after the light was turned off.

"I was delighted when our new R&D department quickly produced a prototype electronic timer that appeared to do everything required. We made a batch of units, which all worked satisfactorily, and I gave the order to change to the new, much improved model. We were soon despatching several thousand units each month to sites throughout the UK. Then we received what we thought was an isolated complaint from a remote part of Scotland. Our units not only didn't turn off, but they were actually turning themselves on without anyone touching a light switch!

"We were sceptical, and arranged for the units to be returned. As we anticipated, they tested out perfectly satisfactorily, but even so, we despatched new units to the far away site in Scotland. They failed again, so, believing there was something peculiar on site, we sent the designer to Scotland.

"Then similar complaints started coming in from other sites and we gradually became submerged under an avalanche of identical complaints from contractors throughout the country.

"We could hardly believe the reason for the fault, discovered by our service engineer while surveying the Scottish dwellings. We had designed and tested our timers by using short runs of cable to simulate room wiring. In practice, long lengths of cable were necessary in a real building, and these caused the room light circuit to possess sufficient electrical capacitance and inductance to trigger the timer circuit.

"We had not done our homework and, in consequence, were unaware of all the criteria that should have been covered in the specification. We were manufacturing a timer that passed all our factory checks, and did everything we expected of it until, that is, the device was installed in a real building.

"The subsequent history is too painful to relate in detail, because we paid very dearly for our lack of quality control. It took several years before we totally cleared the trouble, at very high cost, and much effort was needed to repair damaged relationships. We survived only because we were part of a larger group which supported us during the trauma – a dramatic example of the danger of bad quality and, more particularly, how lack of market research can lead to poor specifications.

"I am sure you will agree when I say that nowadays we would not consider finalising the design of a new product, let alone launching it on the market, without first testing prototypes in *real life* installations. It is a quality policy that pays handsome dividends. It provides the last ditch check on whether you have got it right.

"I understand our experience is rather relative to yours at Linklaters. But we are not alone. It happens, although it should not happen, to many companies.

"Another point is that quality testing applies not only to manufacture.

"An obsession with quality stems from the chief executive. The managing director of Rowntrees, one of the world's great confectioners, speaking at a quality seminar, explained that not only the quality of their famous After Eight mints was meticulously monitored and controlled but there was also quality control of detail. He explained the problems they had in persuading printers to maintain the correct shade of green on the distinctive After Eight carton. To him it was vitally important, because his dictum was *relax in any area, however trivial it may seem, and, inevitably, quality in general will deteriorate.*"

Moss paused for a moment, then continued, "The task of persuading others to move out of what I call the *slough of mediocrity* is one of the major challenges facing you. If you believe in improving quality, as I do, then you must be prepared to nail your colours to the mast and criticise and discard everything that doesn't match up to your expectations.

"My own company, which is approved by the BSI, Quality Assurance Division as a firm of assessed capability, found that it had to impose this quality philosophy on its suppliers, so we involved them in our problems. We invited their engineers to join our production lines, they went into the field with our service engineers, and our quality staff visited their factories. We returned any of their products not measuring up to the specifications.

"Their quality improved. Our buying department records now include suppliers' quality information – reject rates, delivery performance, service breakdowns – information which is essential if we are to maintain, let alone improve, the quality and standards of our own products.

"The importance of effectively communicating with suppliers is equalled by the specification – a benchmark against which we accept or reject a product. The specification, linking as it does the parties by defining exactly what is required of one by the other, is fundamental in the assessment of quality. Unfortunately, writing a good specification, i.e. one which is complete, unambiguous, and really does reflect what is required, demands great skill and information. Since these attributes are rare, poor specifications outnumber good ones; and if a product fails to meet its overall specification in terms of performance, size, life, safety, efficiency, appearance, cost, etc., this failure must be a consequence of poor quality. Now perhaps you can appreciate why the specification is so important and why it is so difficult to draft.

"Once again, I must stress that a product can meet its specification and yet be considered of poor quality, if this specification does not accurately represent what the client requires.

"We have invested time and effort into improving our client relationships. Here are two examples.

"Firstly, we considered the problem of keeping clients up to date with our standard specifications. How could we prevent engineers using out of date technical data when incorporating our equipment into their schemes? It would be impractical and prohibitively expensive to exchange the tens of thousands of catalogues on their shelves each time there was a specification change; and we knew from experience that they would not insert new leaflets if these were simply sent to their offices.

"Our solution was two-pronged. We split our literature into two functions: the selling sections continued to include expensive full-colour presentations, but technical data was excluded from the text. This move, incidentally, allowed us to make the sales presentations more dramatic and punchy. The technical data was carried in well designed, but simple, one-or two-colour leaflets, which were easy to alter and relatively inexpensive to produce.

"The appropriate technical information leaflets are now included with each and every quotation leaving our company. Clients are provided with up to date data when they need it, and this, of course, leads to another benefit as well in ensuring that only correct information is used. This makes it much easier for the engineer to draw in our product.

"There is another bonus. Because the expensive sales leaflets are smaller and rarely need replacing, the new, and far more satisfactory arrangement, saves money.

"Secondly, we introduced a computerised system, which eliminates all the risk of error spoiling our quotations, our main written contacts with clients. Now estimators simply tabulate unit codes and quantities, add a client code, and any special comments. An operator enters this information into a computer through a VDU keyboard, and the machine does the rest.

"Quotations can be multi-addressed by entering further client codes and, if necessary, can be altered line by line at any stage. The machine prints consistent descriptions, extracts correct prices, extends and totals them and, by searching the client and job files, selects the appropriate discounts.

"The system has totally eliminated errors and, from this standpoint alone, has merited the considerable investment in equipment, software, and the preparation of the data base. Again, profit from a quality objective.

"Possibly one point has struck you. I appear to have ignored the group most people instinctively would accuse of poor quality – those who actually make things. After all, if a product performs badly, is poorly finished, or falls to pieces, aren't the workers to blame? The answer is not necessarily, and, in any event, they are rarely completely to blame.

"The product may perform badly. But compared to what? It probably performs as well as its design allows, and no amount of skill on the shop floor will change that! And possibly it breaks down because the design staff were never aware that the product would be used so severely or constantly.

"Production often receives the brickbats for poor quality but usually the fault lies much further back in the chain. Because inspection picks up deficiencies immediately production is completed, it is easy to understand why the blame attaches where it does. But how does one measure the competence and efficiency of staff in the design office, buying department, administration, sales, despatch . . . ? All these people are making decisions, many of them a large number each day, which influence the quality judgements made of your company by your clients. If a delivery is late, the immediate response is to blame production. But how often does the real fault lie with a clerk who gave the client an incorrect despatch date in the first place?

"The real task facing all of us is to extend quality management into the other areas of business, and especially into those where problems are initiated. The executive suites and managers' offices deserve attention. Improve the quality of the groups that always blame others for poor quality, and quality will dramatically improve.

"As the thirty most successful firms in the USA have demonstrated, quality pays, and the chief executive must be obsessive in his seeking to improve it."

Moss sat down to prolonged applause. Time passed quickly during the questions that followed, and the delayed lunch break came while the managers were still eager to hear more of Moss's experiences. He promised to meet them again later.

14 Involvement in quality management

Lunch was a hurried affair, the wives being left to enjoy the sweets while their menfolk returned quickly to the meeting room. As soon as the managers had settled down again, Brennan began, "I'm sorry we were so late for lunch, but the Moss session was worth it, wasn't it?" All the managers nodded their agreement with Brennan's words of praise.

Brennan continued, "We shall now consider various aspects of quality as applicable to Linklaters.

"Our first judgement of a product is often based on eye appeal, but here is a warning. Beware of designers.

"Too often they design for their own pleasure. My cabin, for instance, has been redecorated recently. In appearance it is extremely pleasant – all the switches are correctly positioned for convenience, there are matching curtains and bed covers, splendid fitted furniture, luxurious bathroom, with gold-plated fittings, new showers, a streamlined bath, and sensible cupboard space – but the designer, determined to achieve an even more pleasant appearance, has added wooden trellis work to separate the hand basin from the toilet and bidet. Trellis also covers the facia of the cupboards over the hand basins. All very pleasing in appearance. But the apertures in the trellises are about one and a half inches square, and there are hundreds of them. You can guess the result. They are absolute talcum and dust traps. There's no way the steward can clean them daily.

"What appears, then, to be quality, is not quality at all. So lesson No 1 is that when shown those super colour wash drawings by the designers of room, office, lobby, factory, or any piece of equipment, always check, and recheck, for designers' weaknesses for their own satisfaction.

"Now, I've made the start. I think, Mike, you should continue."

Mike Spurling nodded, and said, "I'll begin with some quality control tasks.

1. We must cut out the jargon associated with quality standards, and make it easy for anyone to understand what is entailed in maintaining quality.
2. Successful problem-solving is the first ingredient in successful quality assurance.
3. Quality management means discovering customer needs and meeting those needs, exactly. It also entails laying down standards for all component parts, and never allowing any deviation from those standards. There must be instruction manuals covering all aspects of production.

"And finally – well, not really finally, but it will do for the time being – quality standards can only be maintained if the chief executive, who is caught up in so many of the company's activities, is willing to give priority to maintaining these quality standards."

He looked at Brennan, but before a reply could be voiced, Laurie Wallace said, "I agree, that is the most important factor. When I was associated with the White Group, before I joined Linklaters, there was the same dedication to quality that we are now discussing. Everyone was obsessed with it. The then managing director, Douglas Clough, drove home the message time and time again. Then came the crunch! They lost a Government contract and Douglas began screaming for reductions in cost, and cuts had to be made. We reduced the number of tests, and demanded a discount from all suppliers. Quality fell, but we got the price right. However, in the long term that didn't solve anything.

"In my opinion, all too often lip service is paid to quality because it is the 'in thing'. So many chief executives like to tell their friends of their determination only to market quality products, but these same executives will quickly decide that quality standards are not all they need to be, if profits fall."

Brennan nodded. "That will definitely not happen so long as I am in charge of Linklaters," he said. "You have my word for it. Carry on Mike."

Spurling said, "I must continue to emphasise the point, because it applies not only to the chief executive, but to all of us – the managers, the work force. We can get tired of maintaining quality, we can begin to compromise; but once we begin compromising, deterioration sets in. We must set, and maintain, our high standards.

"And that's all for the time being."

Brennan turned to Wallace. "Your turn, Laurie," he said.

"To me," Wallace said, "quality means the best value for the price charged – and this applies to everything, from stationery to computers. Quality, then, is when the buyer satisfies his needs at the price he can afford to pay. We have to learn that a salesman can negotiate a price according, perhaps, to the size of an order, but that quality standards are *never* negotiable."

Brennan thanked Wallace and said, "Over to you, Victor."

"Before I became service manager at Linklaters," Clayton said, "I was in a service repair shop at Tallis Vending Machines. It was more of a production unit than a service shop. We found faults, repaired faults, and sometimes corrected designs. We set up what the production manager called a *quality inspectorate*. If there was any possibility of a breakdown, no matter how long after the installation the fault might occur, it was up to the inspectorate to discover the reason.

"I remember one occasion when an inspector tested a coin selector 2,000 times before it failed. The management's decision then was that the selector was not good enough and it had to be improved. That was real quality!

"The result of this monitoring was the identification of problem areas and a statistical analysis showing when justifiable risks could be taken. Spare parts were also earmarked for continual checking after installation.

"Incidentally, there were also wall charts listing all the factors having any bearing on quality. These charts had to be referred to systematically by the testers.

"I was only sorry that with all that experience I couldn't carry out more quality control at Linklaters. With your backing, Bob, I shall be able to do so from now on."

Spurling interrupted, saying, "We must be sensible about quality paper work. When we once had a page or two of data to digest, we now have reams of printouts. But, conversely, sometimes too few records are kept. For example, there should be written instructions for most phases of manufacture. Then there could be no excuse for failure. I've even known drawings not to be updated when changes have taken place, leading, invariably, to faults developing."

Harvey Strong was finding it a little difficult to concentrate as the movement of the ship, ploughing through the water, increased. To him it was very rough indeed; no one else seemed very bothered. He was so tired, too. Their first night on the ship had been a night of love-making for him, with many protestations of affection from Pat. She had won and had an engagement ring to prove it, but she didn't want him to feel that she was now taking him for granted.

Strong's concern was alleviated by the arrival of a steward with coffee. All black was Strong's request.

After the coffee had been cleared, the session recommenced. Laurie Wallace raised his hand like a schoolboy asking for permission to speak. Brennan smiled, nodded to him, and Wallace said, "You asked us to do some research before the meetings. I noted some points I believe are relevant to quality assurance:

1. Quality is sometimes looked upon by employees as a reflection on themselves. Therefore they tend to hide mistakes they have made, or to justify errors. Care should be taken when faults are discovered not to apportion blame, but, by training, to rectify attitudes of mind.

2. No one person has a monopoly of understanding of any particular problem. No one firm has a monopoly of brainpower. We shouldn't be afraid to call in outside consultants to check our standards. The consultants can also help to foresee future problem areas.

3. We must be careful not to create the impression that quality management is just another bandwaggon to jump on. We shall have to explain to the work force that this is no bandwaggon, it is for all time, and it is essential for our survival.

4. Some problems can't be solved except at an uneconomic cost. Provided there is no health or safety factor, the decision has to be made whether to risk production even although the problem has not been solved. We must bear in mind that there will always be some failures – there will always be breakdowns – and on occasion risks must be taken, while the objective is still to maintain quality.

5. The emphasis must also be on pride. If we cannot persuade all our employees to feel proud of the work they are doing, the products they are manufacturing, the services they are giving, then we shall not have an overall success."

Wallace paused and said, "There were two more points, but they have gone from my mind for the moment – which means that the quality of my memory is, temporarily, slipping!"

Brennan said, "I'm sure you'll think of them later, but those were five good points.

"Arising out of problems that can't sometimes be cured, however, I must emphasise that we are not seeking perfection. That is an ideal beyond the reach of most of us.

"Let me give you an example. In my previous company we regularly sent out direct mail shots to offices and shops. We had developed a small unit incorporating our motor, of course, which was ideal for boardrooms, offices, etc. We achieved success with the leaflet, which kept to the formula of *attract attention – arouse interest – stress benefits*. Then one of our managers, an absolute perfectionist and very much quality-minded, told me that the leaflet was very ordinary and certainly did not give any indication of quality. He was allowed a free hand to produce a better leaflet, which he did. It was most attractive, and cost over four times as much as our previous mailing shot. But there was no improvement in the return.

"There you have a case of seeking perfection at a high cost, when a standard quality product was meeting the need. So beware of those people who always want quality plus!

"Finally, we must be prepared to accept criticism, probably the greatest difficulty facing us. Have you ever known a chef agree that some ghastly concoction he has prepared is anything but the finest cuisine? Try returning any item to a shop, after it has been laundered, and complain that it has shrunk; the manager will never agree that it could be the fault of the material, it is always the way it was laundered.

"We're all tarred with the same brush. We can't bear

to think that something we have produced is not perfect. Even when the copiers were breaking down every day, I understand Lundt still insisted that it was because of the way they were being handled – the way they were used, by inefficient staff.

"Managing directors are the worst offenders, they always believe their products are perfect. In fact, many of them dislike the idea of having salesmen to sell them: they consider that customers should queue for their goods. And have you ever known an author to believe a critic? So far as we are concerned, the rule from now on is that our first reaction to criticism is to believe that it is fair."

Spurling said, "I don't want to hog the limelight, but in the main this session is concerned with production. I promise to keep quiet when you start talking about salesmanship . . ."

"I hope you won't!" said Brennan. "The whole idea of this meeting is to have an exchange of views."

"We must expect, and be prepared to meet, the standard problems which will arise when we instigate quality management throughout the group. We must remember that in spite of our efforts, some of the shop-floor workers will still not be interested in turning out better work. We can't sack them, so we must be prepared for a long period of rehabilitation and continual training. The problem with people is that one *against* can influence so many others *for*. And another aspect is that too many supervisors will side with the workers rather than with management. When a minor problem arises, and it could affect production as well as quality, many supervisors will say, "Forget it!" because they don't want to start an argument. We shall have to spend time training our supervisors, and making them realise they are of the utmost importance in management.

"Another aspect is the trade unions. As soon as anything new is introduced their first reaction is, *What's in it for us? Why shouldn't our men get more money for turning out better work?* And so on. We may need a personnel manager to tackle this problem. I'll handle it until then, so long as you all know that it is a problem that must be overcome by discussion, and endless patience.

"Finally, I must repeat that we are all still worried that there may come a time when, with all these problems arising, we may think that investment in quality is too high."

Brennan laughed and said, "What more can I say? Of course I shall think the investment is too high, but I'll keep telling myself that it is an investment for the future. And cross my heart, I promise you I'll see it through whatever the cost! It might be a good thing to read out to you what Reg Spencer, Quality Improvement Manager of Rolls-Royce has to say on the subject."

Brennan took a newspaper cutting from his pocket and read:

"In today's industrial climate there appears to be a preoccupation with job security when, in fact, customer security is, by my standards, more important. With the best product in the world, be it a washing machine or a motor car, we cannot survive if nobody wants to buy it.

"Job security would be a natural successor to customer satisfaction. That stems from a product or service which displays fitness for purpose and value for money. And that could only be achieved by *total* quality control throughout the company.

"Everybody has got to be involved with quality. It has got to start at the top and cascade down to the shop floor . . ."

"And Mike, after only brief meetings with the shop floor employees I think they will all be very eager to be a part of a quality campaign."

Victor Clayton, who somehow felt he was not making the right impression on Brennan, said, "We know that quality management simply means conformance with standards without necessarily adding to costs. The snag is that in the service department we are always advocating prevention methods while quality circles etc. are more concerned with cures. Ask any of our service engineers for their views, and they will tell you that they are up against faults which could have been prevented by earlier action. I suggest, therefore, that in the first place I call a meeting of our service engineers and ask them to give details of all breakdowns they believe could have been prevented. These engineers can play one of the most important parts of all in quality control – they really do know the problems. You talked before about no one accepting criticism. I don't want to criticise you, Mike, but the fact is that so often when a service engineer complains, he is written off as 'just another moaner'. His views are rarely accepted."

"The same applies to salesmen," said Harvey Strong. "They meet the customers, They, too, know what's wrong. But those in the production line are always criticising salesmen for demands which can't be met. There must be a get-together of salesmen, service staff, and production, to thrash out these things. We must stop this 'them and us' attitude, which is so prevalent in most companies I have known."

Spurling interrupted, "That's hardly fair –"

"Hold on," said Brennan, "remember, our first reaction to criticism is going to be to accept it."

"OK," said Mike, "I'll accept it. But our problems in the past were that we knew what was wrong but without being disloyal to the board we couldn't give any reasons."

"Some excuse!" murmured Strong to himself.

"I understand," Brennan said, "but let me once again list some of our objectives:

1. Ensure that every manager is a quality fanatic, each and every one must be committed to the task of inspiring the employees of Linklaters also to be quality enthusiasts.
2. Richard will prepare budgets so that we shall all know the costs.
3. Arrange training for inspectors and supervisors. To save delay it may be as well to arrange for outside training courses to cover this need.
4. Set target dates for completion of objectives.
5. Reintroduce the suggestion box for a limited time before the quality circles commence. We can award prizes then for good suggestions, which can be discussed later at the circle meetings.
6. Review all procedures every three months."

"The usual time taken to reach quality targets can be eighteen months to two years. Our target is six to nine months. You will now all have gathered what we are trying to achieve in these seminars: *inspiring each other to introduce every aspect of quality control in our respective spheres.*"

The steward entered the room and served tea, but the discussion continued.

15 Quality circles

After tea, Brennan opened the day's final session, saying, "You will remember that I suggested that you should all make a study of quality circles, to enable you to add your contributions to this session. Mike has a full understanding of the principles and practices, and so has Laurie. When quality circles first became popular in our country, I immediately became deeply interested, so much so that I visited Japan. I was shown great courtesy and a willingness on the part of the Japanese to explain how quality circles had improved every aspect of their production. They didn't seem so interested, however, in any of the other directions in which quality circles could apply.

"I believe implicitly, as you know, in innovation. It's a thrill for me when a new concept is suggested, but the rational side of my mind insists that I make allowances for this enthusiasm and emotional involvement, and make a thorough investigation. This I did with quality circles. Laurie mentioned gimmicky innovations – bandwaggons on to which so many academics jump, and for which so many managers fall. T Groups, transactional analysis, all kinds of grids – the A Theory, the B Theory, right through the alphabet theories – all these bandwaggons do some good, by arousing enthusiasm if nothing else. They also give some managers something new to cling to.

"My visit to Japan convinced me that the Japanese had

found a winner for themselves. To the Japanese, the word of a manager is a command, not to be argued with or disputed in any way. Therefore, the thought that a worker could, during a discussion period, put forward ideas that were contrary to convention was at one time unthinkable. When, therefore, it was decided that every worker at a factory was responsible for quality, the next obvious move was to form discussion groups, and these, as you know, they called Quality Circles.

"The Japanese once had a reputation for producing inferior products, so the concept of quality improvement to enable them to compete even more strongly against the rest of the world was to them a winner. In other countries quality circles proliferated with varying success, the reason for failure being that miracles were expected of them by management, while the shop-floor workers were convinced that it was just another ploy to improve productivity, and to bring about more mechanisation to cut labour costs. However, that period is now almost over and there is new vigour in the drive for quality, of which quality circles form a part. One of the reasons why the idea has become more successful is that we now realise that a quality circle is simply a meeting of people with a common purpose. Also, unlike the Japanese, British quality circles now operate in spheres other than productivity, and that, too, is our aim.

"But I've spoken long enough on the subject. If each of us keeps his contribution short, we can cover a wide area. Will you make a start, Mike?"

Spurling said, "I would state categorically that Quality Circles is only another name for problem-solving groups."

Brennan said, "Why, then, did the Japanese use the terminology *quality circles* and not *problem-solving circles*?"

Wallace replied, "I have no great knowledge of the Japanese work force, but I can imagine the reaction of some British workers to an invitation to volunteer for problem-solving circles! Their response could well be, 'Let them do their own bloody problem-solving!'

"But if the invitation is for them to help improve the quality of the product, something which would give them a certain amount of pride, they would react differently. It's all a matter of psychology. To tell their families or friends that they were members of a quality circle would win some acclamation. To claim that they were on a team to solve problems would be met by ribald remarks."

There was general agreement with Wallace's explanation, and Brennan said, "Shall we get enough volunteers for the circles? Should we consider some type of reward for the members? Are the teams likely to run out of ideas quickly? Mike, what do you think?"

Spurling said, "There is a theory that all workers hate their work. That is only usually true when there is a 'them and us' syndrome. I've found that most people, even if they don't love their work, don't hate it either. But it depends so much on management. An unhappy work force is nearly always due to bad management. In most factories and offices the work forces are anxious to co-operate.

"I don't want to beat the drum, but they're as good as any others anywhere, and I've been to a few places overseas, as you know.

"I'm sure we shall have no problem finding volunteers. Participation is the key to the future success not only of Linklaters but of British industry as a whole.

"Now on to your second point. No, we can't introduce a payment or bonus system. The unions would be up in arms and it would cause bad feeling in the work force generally. In addition, we should get volunteers for the wrong reasons.

"And as for your third point, I think you'll find that there will be no shortage but a flood of ideas for discussion."

Hemmings asked, "How do we form a circle?"

"I shall call a meeting, or several meetings if need be," Brennan answered, "and explain the objectives of quality circles. I shall impress on everyone that if these circles are to be successful, the result can only be more job security and higher incomes. I'll do my best to inspire them. After the meetings, each of the employees will be given an explanatory booklet detailing the meaning of quality control and quality circles."

Brennan continued, reading now from notes, "This is the outline of the ground I shall be covering when I address the meetings: .

1. Details of the reason for introducing quality circles, and emphasis that, to succeed, we must improve the quality of our products.
2. Each circle we introduce will comprise four to eight employees.
3. There will be meetings for all 'circle' volunteers, to explain how these circles will be conducted, and training sessions to cover leadership.
4. Training will also be given in problem-solving.
5. The meetings will be held during working time, and will be of about one hour's duration. They will be held each week for the first four weeks, and later once every two months or so.
6. Within these circles there will be complete equality between all employees.
7. One person only, the leader, will be responsible for the efficient running of the circle, and will present the results of the discussions to the quality manager.
8. It will be emphasised that the objective of each member of a circle is to use his own skills and creativity to improve the quality of work.
9. There will be no pressure on anyone to join a circle.
10. It will not be looked upon as an elitist body, nor will the participants be kept separate from their work-mates.

11. Each volunteer will receive a booklet giving full details of what membership of a quality circle entails. Only after reading this booklet will we ask him for a decision as to whether he wishes to join the circle or not."

Brennan put the notes away and said, "Following a time for questions, I'll point out that in the past they have all used such phrases as 'They'll never listen to me' or 'It's like talking to a brick wall.' Now we shall listen to them.

"I'll finish on an inspiring note, but in the main I'm going to deal with facts, and nothing is so impressive as the truth when it is recognised as such. That's about it, as far as the initial meeting of employees is concerned. Any questions?"

Hemmings said, "Won't an hour away from the production line affect production and prove costly? And won't some of the work force feel that if we can afford to lose that time, why don't we pay them more as an incentive to produce better quality goods?"

Brennan answered, "Mike has assured me that he can organise in such a way that, to begin with, one hour a week will not affect production, although it would do if it were to be continued on a weekly basis. He also feels confident of being able to explain to the work force the importance to them of the circles, and of asking them, too, to ensure that no productivity is lost."

Hemmings shrugged his shoulders and said, "I'd need to be convinced of that! But how will the others feel about some of the work force having a break, if it's looked on as a break?"

Spurling answered, "I can't give you any proof, obviously, but the members of the quality circles are going to have to work hard – damned hard. This is what they'll soon be telling their fellow men, and many of the workers will say they'd rather be on the bench than have to be subjected to the questioning, probing discussions of the quality circles. I can assure you, Richard, there is no problem. And they'll also all be eager to put forward their own ideas for discussion by the circles."

Clayton asked, "How are you going to pick your leaders? Will they all be survivors, inspectors, assistant works manager . . .?"

Again Spurling answered, "I know my team well. I know those who believe they can lead, those who don't want to lead, and those who think they can lead but can't. Again, there'll be no problem, because very few of the work force will want to take the responsibility of leadership and controlling the circles. I would suggest we appoint a leader in the first place for six months."

Hemmings said, "Who decides on the times of the quality circles meetings? And where will they be held?"

"As far as production is concerned, obviously it is Mike who will decide," said Brennan, "until we appoint our quality manager. I don't think we need decide now where the meetings are to be held."

Strong said, "And who will decide on the subjects to be discussed at these circle meetings?"

Spurling answered, "At the first meeting there will be a brainstorming session so that all the members can have the opportunity of voicing their feelings. From then on the leaders will decide on the agendas, in co-operation with management."

Wallace asked, "And how will the reporting system work?"

Brennan answered, "The best plan is for us to issue some report forms, which can be completed after each meeting. The first entry on the form would obviously be the problem under discussion. Then can follow the decisions made or the reasons for postponing a decision until a further meeting can be held. Several solutions may be suggested, and there must be space for each of these on the forms. It may be that, because of costs, management will have to refer the matter back to the circle. Finally, there must be space for the action decided upon. At the following meetings the minutes of the previous meeting will be read, discussed, and further action decided upon if necessary. There must also be space for a feedback from management."

"Could the problem arise," asked Hemmings, "of a 'them and us' syndrome? In the circles they will be all chiefs, while outside the circles they will all be Indians."

Brennan interrupted, "We did discuss this previously, and Mike said he could see no problem."

"Sorry," said Hemmings. "I remember now – I had forgotten for the moment."

"But it bears repeating," said Brennan, "because a great deal of the success of the circles will depend on those who don't volunteer but still feel they can play a part in the improvement of the quality of our products and services."

Wallace said, "I think, possibly, I'm the only one here who has had some practical experience of quality circles. One of the problems at the earlier meetings is that everyone wants to change everything. When no action is taken, they become disillusioned."

"Laurie," interrupted Brennan, "if you had that problem previously, then the leadership was bad. If we choose the wrong leaders, we must expect difficulties. Our training in leadership must be so efficient that this particular problem will not arise."

"Quite right," said Wallace. "I didn't make my point clearly, but I agree, if the leadership training is effective, the problem should be overcome."

"Who will train the leaders?" asked Strong.

"Until we appoint a training manager, you will!" answered Brennan.

"Good! I'll look forward to that." Strong was pleased that his teaching abilities had been recognised. He was the only one of the managers who had conducted training courses.

Hemmings said, "All volunteers will be given leadership training, although they are not all going to become leaders. And will they also be attending a problem-solving course?"

"Yes," said Brennan.

"And who will run that?"

"In the first place, I shall," said Brennan. "I seem to have spent most of my life solving problems. However, as soon as possible, I shall hand the job over to someone else."

"To a training manager?" asked Wallace.

"You're right to pick me up on that," said Brennan. "I didn't mention a training manager earlier, because, ideally, every manager should be able to train his staff. The course we shall need for managers, therefore, will be a 'training the trainer' course."

Clayton said, "As I see it, we've covered most of the areas associated with quality circles, but action must always be seen to be taken by both those in the circles and those outside them. If action cannot be taken, the full reason must be given. Who, in the first place, will be ensuring that action is taken? Will it be you, Bob?"

"No. I think it will have to be Laurie Wallace, for the overall group. As far as production is concerned. Mike will have to be responsible for seeing that action is taken."

Wallace said, "I can assure you that I shall be deeply concerned with all circles other than production."

"You'll have to be mighty tough, Laurie," said Spurling. "It won't be as cut and dried as you imagine; too much of it will be concerned with spending money. That always happens in the initial stages. However, as far as I am concerned it will be quite straightforward. It's problems in manufacturing which will have to be solved to improve the quality."

Brennan said, "There is one factor we must all remember: we are all human, and often the circle may come up against a problem, the solving of which we should have thought of first. By 'we' I really mean you, Mike. Something within us, when this arises, resists the idea put forward only because we didn't think of it first."

"That won't apply to me," said Spurling.

"I'm sure it won't," said Brennan. "But I think it's worth mentioning. And that's it, for today."

They talked for a short while about the QE2, and the various activities available for the enjoyment of the passengers.

Clayton said, "There's a film we want to see; we're going to the cinema."

The Hemmings had decided to play bridge, which, thought Strong, was typical of them.

Strong and Pat were going to try out a new system at the casino, which, thought Hemmings, was typical of them.

The Spurlings intended visiting the Queen's Room to watch a hypnotist act, while the Wallaces, who loved dancing, were going to spend the evening moving around from one dance area to another.

Brennan decided he would spend the early part of the evening checking the notes he had written, and had duplicated, on conducting quality circle meetings.

16　The mole

It was two am when Brennan and Vivienne returned to their cabin. Viv loved dancing, Brennan did not, so they had compromised and only danced until one-forty-five instead of two am.

Brennan asked, "What do you think of the wives?"

Viv answered, "We've only been together a day or so, and then not all the time."

"But, darling, you're so perceptive," he paused, "except, of course, of my weaknesses!"

She laughed and said, "You haven't any." Then she continued, "Dorothy Wallace is a very overpowering woman. She dominates Laurie, but does that really matter?"

"It might or it might not," said Brennan. "It all depends on how much the domination carries over into his business life. The psychologist Wilbur Burke gives three reasons for a woman dominating her husband. The first is that she was born with a strong personality and always dominated her parents by shouting the house down if she didn't get what she wanted. The second is that some men like being dominated, and they turn their wives into dominating persons. The third is that the husband is a weak character, and the wife feels that only by domination can she urge him on to better things."

Viv asked, "Under which heading would you put Dorothy?"

"I don't know yet, but if it is the last, as I suspect it is,

that Wallace is quite a weak person underneath his
extrovert manner, then Dorothy's domination can turn
him into a better manager. A great deal must depend on
how much he tells her about his business problems. If he
tells her too much, she'll be likely to give advice, and,
without her knowing the full facts, that advice could be
wrong. The man does have ability, but outside pressures
could affect him in the long term. For example, dominating wives nearly always consider their husbands are
undervalued and underpaid, and that could be a long-
term problem. Furthermore, he drinks too much, but
that again needn't affect his work in the short term."

Vivienne said, "I'm hungry. Let's have some tea and
sandwiches."

"What a good idea!" Brennan pressed the bell and the
night steward quickly appeared, took the order, and soon
returned with tea and chicken sandwiches.

"You're lucky," said Vivienne, "you don't need much
sleep. I shall stay in bed until ten o'clock, but you'll have
to be up by seven-thirty."

"Don't rub it in," said Brennan, "I made the rules. I
bet they're cussing me for working them so hard. But it'll
test their mettle. What do you think of Pat Moore?"

"I saw the way she looked at you, and the way you ran
your eyes all over her!"

"And that influences you?"

"Not at all! Any normal man would look twice at Pat."
Then she added, "I like her. I believe she's a very nice
girl – and she's no fool, either! All the young officers
make a beeline for her as soon as she appears, and she
brushes them all off so sweetly. I really do believe she
loves that great teddy bear, Harvey Strong. I think she'll
be a very good influence on him. But why can't you get
away from business for five minutes?"

"It's the way I'm built. That's why I'm successful,
when others fail. You know, Viv, I've met many men of
quality who should have succeeded but didn't. I've also

met men without the asset of all-round quality who have succeeded because they never gave up trying to achieve their objectives. What I'm looking for is men of quality who are also men of high endeavour, who never give up."

"I heard you say that in a speech."

"You must have heard all my views twice over, or more."

"But I do like hearing them," said Viv.

"That's why I love you, you're so sensible."

"What a dreadful word – sensible!"

"All right, you're sexy as well. Does that satisfy you?"

Vivienne said, "But can you really expect someone like Harvey Strong to dedicate most of his spare time to thinking of ways of improving the company's affairs?"

"He's a manager, isn't he?"

"But it isn't his business. He won't make the huge profits that you will, if you sell the business."

"That," said Brennan, "is the standard argument of many managers working for medium sized companies. It doesn't arise at all with the giants of industry – the ICIs, the IBMs, Beecham's – because there even the chairman is a paid employee, so the managers don't relate the profitability of the company to their personal incomes. Provided they get reasonable rises, they're quite content. And incidentally, Viv, I would still be dedicated to success, even if I were an employee. The profit of the company wouldn't concern me, so long as it was doing well. Everyone can't reach the top – there isn't room – and probably 80 per cent of managers don't want that extra responsibility anyway. It's the men who decide that dedication is not really worthwhile who are always envious of the success of others.

"You see what you've done, Viv, don't you? You've got me going, and now I'm making speeches to you. It's time we went to bed. But just before we do, how about Penny Hemmings?"

"I think she's very fond of her husband but she loves

herself most. She wants them both to be something. If her husband were knighted, she would be in seventh heaven. But I think they're a good team. She keeps telling us all how brilliant her husband is – what a financial genius, etc. – so that's something in her favour. Is he a financial genius?"

"Genius is a much misused word. He's highly efficient, but I'm not sure of his loyalty. He wasn't very loyal to Linklaters when he was trying to persuade me to take over. He could have made his arguments just as valid without being so derogatory about the rest of the board."

Vivienne yawned, apologised, and said, "I really do like Mary Clayton and Tina Spurling though. And Tina is a very clever girl, too. I'm sure she'll be a great help to her husband."

She stood up and began to undress. "Are you really going to make them all directors?" she asked.

The answer was a shrug of Brennan's shoulders.

It was eight am on Thursday. Brennan had decided to cut out breakfast and have tea and toast in the cabin. He knew he was weak-willed so far as good food was concerned, and the breakfast menu in the Queen's Grill was a match for many a restaurant's dinner offerings. There was too much to resist, and Brennan felt that two slices of dry toast would have to sustain him until lunchtime. Whether at home or abroad, Vivienne always had the same breakfast – cereal and fruit juice.

About to pick up a piece of toast from the plate, Brennan paused as the telephone bell rang. Vivienne, in the bed nearest to the telephone, picked up the receiver. She said, "Yes, he's here, who wants him?" Then, "Hold on please."

Brennan looked enquiringly at his wife.

"It's a personal call for you, Bob. The radio office was checking that you would be available to accept the call. It may be due in the next ten minutes or so."

Brennan said, "It can only be Cathy. Tell them I'll stay here until the call comes through."

When she had relayed the message and replaced the receiver, Brennan said, "I left strict instructions that if I was needed the call had to go through Cathy. I can trust her to stop anyone contacting me on trivial matters. My view is that if a department can't run efficiently for a week or so without the managers, there's something wrong."

Vivienne said, "Then it must be something important."

"I'd say so. Let's see, Cathy Lipman must have been with me for seven years now, and she knows what action is needed. She wouldn't trouble me unnecessarily."

The toast remained uneaten, the cereal untouched.

The bell rang again. This time Brennan grabbed the receiver.

"Mr Brennan?"

"Yes."

"I have a call for you."

The next moment Brennan heard Cathy's voice.

"Mr Brennan?"

"Yes, Cathy, what's the problem?"

"I wouldn't have bothered you, but – "

"OK. What is it?"

"One of your managers is a mole," said Cathy dramatically.

"A what?"

"One of them is working for Canada Copiers."

Brennan's stomach churned and his heart beat faster, but he said calmly enough, "Start at the beginning, Cathy, and be brief."

"The European managing director of Canada Copiers is, as you know, Mark Cornell. He recently sacked his personnel manager, Donald Powell. That same Donald Powell telephoned to speak to you. I told him you were away; he said he must get in touch with you, as it was

most important for the future of Linklaters. He told me
he knew you were on the QE2 and I said I was your
personal assistant and would relay any message to you. It
was late last evening, about seven o'clock, when he
telephoned.

"He sounded as though he had been drinking.
Luckily, I was still at the office. He said – and these are
his words, I took them down – 'That bastard Mark
Cornell has taken on one of your managers who is now
doing his best to entice away two other managers from
Linklaters.''

Brennan wasted no time on needless comment. "Why
didn't you 'phone me last evening?"

"I did try, but there were problems getting through."

"Right! Did Powell say anything else?"

"No."

"Why didn't he name the defector?"

"He said he didn't know his name. It had all been very
much hush-hush, and although he was personnel
manager, he had been kept in the dark. He said he found
out what was happening quite by chance – he didn't tell
me what that chance was."

Brennan took a deep breath, thought for a moment,
then said, "Anything else, Cathy?"

"No. Isn't that enough?"

"Don't worry, Cathy," Brennan said. "Everything will
be all right."

"I'm sorry they spoiled your break."

"It's hardly a break!"

"Mr Powell said he would call you on the QE2 if you
wanted to speak to him. I think he probably feels you'll
give him a job."

"That won't be necessary, and anyway I don't want
him. He must have been sacked on the spot. I wonder
why. I know of him though. He's a near alcoholic. If he
had any more information, he would have told you.
Thanks Cathy, see you Monday."

Brennan replaced the receiver and sat staring at it for a few moments, thinking hard. Vivienne didn't interrupt his thoughts. Then he smiled and said, "Nothing ever goes smoothly for long."

"What happened?" asked his wife.

Brennan told her.

"What will you do?" she asked.

"Nothing! Absolutely nothing! I'll carry on as if the telephone call hadn't come through. I shall think, I shall ask questions, I shall plan on how to knock Canada Copiers to hell and back."

"I wonder why that man did it. Why does he want our people?"

"That's simple! For all its faults, Linklaters did make a hole in the market. Canada Copiers are, of course, a Canadian company, but their biggest growth has been in Europe. They were having problems when they appointed Mark Cornell managing director. He's a New Yorker, renowned for his toughness. There's a story told that he was once having breakfast with a friend, a director, who said to him almost casually, 'I was wondering about my future.' Cornell is reputed to have replied, 'If you're wondering about your future, you don't have one with us. You're fired!'

"Obviously he's sacked Powell for some reason or other, and Powell wants to get his own back. That happens time and time again. How else does the taxman find out about so many misdemeanours? A managing director must be whiter than white, or else very secretive, or he would never be able to sack anyone without worrying about a come-back."

"But the Cornell man didn't worry about that?"

"No. He probably thought Powell knew nothing about it."

"But, Bob, you're known as a very tough business-man."

"Right enough! But there's a great difference between

being tough and being ruthless. Cornell is ruthless. I never liked him, and he certainly doesn't like me! We were both speakers at a conference once. We didn't gel."

"Surely he isn't doing this from vindictiveness?"

"No, although with him I wouldn't be too sure. I believe he knows that under my guidance Linklaters will be a strong competitor; he thought Linklaters were finished, leaving his company as the only manufacturer with a sort of British background. All the main competitors are either Japanese or American.

"Canada Copiers can do without us on the market. Besides, Cornell would like to know our plans for the future. He knows the score, too, so far as our people are concerned. He's well aware of what a great job they did under very difficult conditions, and one of his problems is that he lacks good management. He knows, too, that we'll get the product right, although he doesn't yet know how. And it's almost impossible for us to replace key men quickly."

"What a horrible man! But isn't there some law about passing on secrets?"

"Yes, there is. But it's difficult to uphold. By the time court action is taken, it's usually not worthwhile."

"But who is the mole, do you think? They all seem so nice. I was only thinking last evening what a splendid team you have; they appear to be so loyal, even in these early days."

"Let's not worry about them. My first objective is to carry on as usual, to try to impress the vacillators. It could be that I can win them over, and we'd only lose one man – the mole. I could manage with the loss of one person, whoever it was. Viv, I always knew they all had alternatives in mind. They would have to, with all the bother at Linklaters. One of them, or more, could have approached Canada Copiers, for all I know. But I have an idea that Cornell approached one of them first, probably through a head hunter.

"Now, to be objective, let us assume that Powell has given us the correct information. What are the problems?

"If Spurling goes, there will be a production problem.

"If Clayton goes, I shall have no one to reorganise service.

"If Strong goes, I shall be hard put to find an instant replacement.

"I could do without Wallace, but even without him there would be a problem in the short term with running the quality control.

"If Hemmings went, that wouldn't be a serious blow.

"Look, it's a setback. If the worst happens, I shall have to invest more cash, I shall have to smooth over Scott & Ballinger, and there will be a time lag during which losses could be quite heavy. But I'll pull through, there's no question about that!"

"Will you be able to face the men at your meeting, knowing what's going on?"

"Of course I shall! So far as I'm concerned, they're all innocent, except one, so the majority are on my side.

"It may be that I've already given the defector food for thought. Who knows?"

"You've already given him a lot of information he can pass on," said Vivienne.

Brennan sighed. "Maybe you're right, at that!"

17 On meetings

None of the managers could have had any idea of Brennan's traumatic experience from his manner on entering the meeting room.

There was the usual banter, then Brennan said, "This morning you will discuss quality-circle meetings and how best to conduct them. To help you, I have written some notes on the subject.

"What I want you to do is to add to, delete, or elaborate on these notes, so that we can soon complete a section of a quality-circle training manual.

"Here are the notes. I'll leave you to it, and hear your verdicts and opinions later."

Brennan handed out the notes and swiftly left the room.

PRINCIPLES OF QUALITY CIRCLE LEADERSHIP

1. A group leader is also a manager. As a leader, his duty is to guide and motivate the group to give of its best. As a group manager he must:
   * carefully prepare for each meeting with such basic checking as:
     - right number of chairs available,
     - ashtrays,
     - pens, paper, drawings, charts,

  – possibly overhead projectors, computers, cameras, etc.,
* define the objective of the meeting,
* plan the agenda,
* determine the time to be allowed for each subject,
* ensure that all the information has been, or will be, made available to all members of the group.

2. The leader must be taught not to expect immediate results. It may take time for the group to work as a team.

3. The leader will use standard questioning techniques. These are:
   * *The Open Question*
     "Tell us, Bill, your views on this new design." "Explain more fully, John, how you overcame that problem."
   * *The Closed Question*
     "But did you, Henry, join the terminals?" "Will you be able to get agreement on that point, Fred?"
   * *The Appealing Question*
     "You all know that it's in the best interests of the company that we agree on this new testing operation, and you all know it's the right thing to do; you will be letting yourselves and your team mates down if we don't get agreement now. Can I have a show of hands?"
   * *The Check Question*
     "Harry, what was the formula we used at that time?" "John, will you work that out on your calculator and see if we've got it right."
   * *The General Question*
     "Now let us discuss the question of the automatic louvres and the infiltration of oil. How do you see it, Donald? Or would you prefer someone else to make a start?"

* *The Direct Question*
  "We can't play around any longer, we have to make a decision now. What is your decision?"

4. The leader's opening remarks must ensure that the group fully understands the subject, the purpose of the discussion, and the parameters within which they can work.

5. It may be that a part which has proved faulty in constant use is one of the subjects for discussion. The leader should, then, ask the persons who have been most affected, or know most about the subject, to give their views. General discussion can follow.

6. The leader maintains control at all times, without causing discord. During the meeting he:
   * Prevents individuals from monopolising the discussion, and remembers that he, too, should not believe his position entitles him to talk more than anyone else.
   * Ensures that all the necessary notes are taken.
   * Makes certain that everyone has an equal opportunity to state his views.
   * Makes certain that everyone understands all the points being made. This should be checked by continual questioning, and repetition of points if necessary.
   * Tries to prevent members interrupting others.
   * Prevents valueless discussion and digressions.
   * Never embarrasses any member of the circle.
   * Avoids direct criticism of members. If criticism has to be made, it should be done before or after the meeting, and in private.
   * Never ridicules ideas, no matter how foolish they may appear to be. They are never foolish to the person who originates them.
   * Regularly summarises throughout the session.
   * Always strives for a consensus, but if that is not feasible, is prepared to accept a majority decision,

and makes this point known quite early in the meeting.

Know Your Members

People don't change because they become members of a quality circle, but one thing they should have in common is a determination to improve the quality of a product or service, or the running of a department.

The leader must always include himself if there is criticism of the personality, habits, or manners of those in the circle. If, for example, he is a compulsive talker, he will be a very inefficient leader. If he is quick-tempered, he cannot carry out his task satisfactorily. He should not be intolerant or have any prejudices so far as the circle is concerned. Most leaders will be chosen because they have shown the right qualities of leadership. It is, therefore, up to the leader to know how to get the best out of the members of the circle.

Here are some of the problem men and women who will, undoubtedly, be found in most circles:

The compulsive talker.
The silent listener.
The reminiscent member.
The team bigot.
The timid member.
The overbearing member.
The blamer.

If a circle comprises eight members, possibly only a couple will come under any of the above headings. The majority of volunteers will be reasonable people, who will give and take. Sometimes they may argue, sometimes they will be amenable, but that is how we all act. A team of 'yes' men is of no use to anyone, but the leader must know how to handle the one or two difficult members he will find in his circle.

The compulsive talker

There is, no doubt, a psychological reason for a person to be a compulsive talker, but I'm no psychologist. Why do some people talk, and talk – and talk – and never seem to know that they are boring us?

There is no use even suggesting indirectly that they are talking too much. They won't believe you are referring to them.

They think that every word they utter is a word of wisdom, and everyone wants to hear their views. The only solution is to interrupt.

At some time when he pauses for breath, or to glance at some notes, or even hesitates for a fraction of a second, the leader must say, 'That's a good point you've made,' and turn to someone else, saying, 'Now, Tom, I want your views,' or 'Let's hear what someone else thinks'.

The leader can do this as often as he likes, because the compulsive talker will never realise the reason for the interruptions. He is already getting ready for the next avalanche of words. But for all this weakness, he can be a useful member of the circle.

The silent listener

This type of person often has a great deal to offer, but it is sometimes due to shyness that he sits listening, and says so little. It is up to the leader to ask continually for his advice or his opinion. If he is a technical man, it is quite easy to defer to his judgement, to build him up, and so eliminate some of his shyness.

The reminiscent member

This man lives in the past. He can only think of the good old days when the products were either stronger or weaker, better or worse, or the management was much better or much worse. It doesn't really matter. He can always harp back and tell a story.

You can always recognise him by his repetition of "You wouldn't have got Mr Tom or Mr Henry to do that kind of thing", referring to late directors or managers; or

"He should have been here years ago. I remember when I only had . . ."; or "I had to get to work every day before some of these so-and-so's are even up!"

Whatever the problem that crops up, Mr Reminiscent will recall some apt story from the past, to prove that everything is wrong nowadays.

All this must be pre-empted by the leader. He may say, "Eric, of course, has a long experience of the problems we are now facing. But let us forget the past for the moment. Tell us, Eric, what is your current opinion of . . ."; or "Eric will be the first to admit that it's no use harking back to the past. We have to live with the problem now. So, Eric, start us off with your viewpoint."

The team bigot

He is a difficult fellow! He never believes that he can ever be wrong about anything. To every new suggestion he will answer, "You can't do it that way, it won't work. In all my experience there is no way you can join F and N in a direct line"; or "This may appear too complex for some of you, but I know that . . .", followed by jargon that is only understandable by those who have high technical qualifications. He can never state things in simple language.

The team bigot is far better at destroying than building. For all that, he does have a great deal of knowledge, and it is up to the leader to persuade him to explain in the simplest language what he believes can be achieved.

He can say, "Harry, we're not as clever as you, so just keep it simple."

Once he believes that his technical skills are recognised by all, he will often not be quite so dogmatic.

The timid member

He probably only volunteered to join the quality circle because his wife nagged him to do so. He is easily shouted down, and rarely stands up for himself, but the leader must protect him in the early days – fight his battles for him – encourage him to stand by his views, and congratulate him when he does so.

The overbearing member

This one shouts a lot, and he can also be a table thumper. He believes that the louder the voice, the more certain it will be that the circle will accept his views. Between meetings the leader must tell him that he is a very strong person with a strong personality, but would he please help him – the leader – by giving others a break. Because of his strength, they may not want to argue with him, when arguing might bring about the best results.

The leader can say something like this: "Do me a favour, Bill, take it easy will you – keep your voice down. I know you feel strongly about some things which the others may perhaps have got wrong, but we do have to work as a team, don't we?"

Like the compulsive talker, he is also incurable, but he may be held in check for short periods.

The blamer

Another person who will rarely admit he is wrong. If a machine breaks down, it is due to lack of investment by the company. If absenteeism increases, it is because of company policy of pressurising the work force. Designs are wrong, computer programmes are wrong – in fact, there isn't much right with anything.

For all that, he is usually extremely good at solving problems where no blame can possibly attach to himself.

If the leader is known as a stickler for factual evidence – evidence which cannot be denied – this will often spike the guns of the persistent blamer. When he comes to appreciate the fairness of the leader, he will, to a certain degree, change his ways.

Again, a reminder that these problem members are in the minority, but the leader must be aware of what he may be up against, and know how to handle any contingency which may arise through an individual's idiosyncrasies.

The leader must not imagine that a shop-floor worker is any different from a member of a board of directors. At directors' meetings there can be the same problem people as at quality circles.

CONCLUSION OF MEETING

1. Full notes must be taken, and read back to the circle for agreement. These will subsequently be typed and again shown to the circle members so that there can be no misunderstanding.
2. The minutes of the meeting – decisions arrived at, decisions postponed – must be listed and sent to the quality manager.
3. The minutes of the meeting, and decisions made, will be read at the following meeting before the new subjects are discussed.

Possibly the success of quality management will depend on these meetings, because they are problem-solvers. If they fail, the objectives will not be achieved. If they are reasonable, the quality performance of the company will be reasonable. But if these quality circles, under good leaders, perform outstandingly, as most of them will, then our objectives will most certainly be reached.

The managers pleased Wallace by appointing him the circle leader. Then they got down to trying to improve on Brennan's work.

18   The trap

When Brennan left the meeting room, he intended to find a quiet spot to enable him to relax and plan. Walking past the shops, he smiled to himself as he realised that the following afternoon session was on problem-solving. Here was he, facing a major problem, which could have been the ideal example for a case study.

He approached the Queen's room, where preparations were being made for the *walk-about-talk-about* by a famous French film star. The programme stated that he would tell background stories and would also answer questions. Already many seats had been filled by blue-rinsed matrons, determined to be near their idol – all ready to ask really personal questions.

Brennan about turned and walked upstairs to the Double Two room, where the designer had an affinity with red. But the effect was of brightness, and on the dance floor were the gorgeous Sweet Elegance dancers, wearing tights and long woollen leg-warmers, rehearsing for the evening show.

Brennan climbed the spiral staircase, walked once more past the shops, to the door leading to the Signals deck. At the top of the stairs the wind was so strong that he had difficulty opening the door. On the deck there were chairs under cover and offering some protection from the wind.

No sooner had Brennan seated himself, than a steward appeared with two blankets, one for the lower half of his body, and the other to put around his shoulders. Suddenly he felt warm and snug, and completely relaxed. "Nothing like life at sea, whatever the weather," he remarked to the steward.

"That's right, sir – but it is cold. We shall be serving bouillon at eleven, but if you'd like a nice hot cup of coffee now I can soon get it for you."

"No thanks, I'm OK."

Brennan's mind was already concentrating on the problems. First, how to find the defector. Then, how to head off any others who might want to defect – that was, if there were any others. And if so, had they already been approached? Had they agreed to further talks, or had they refused outright?

He finally considered the possibility of them all leaving.

Very remote, he decided. But he remembered again the old adage *never be shocked – never be surprised*. If that should happen, he decided, he personally would take control of marketing, sales, and finance.

He would then find the best people available to take over, temporarily, production and service. He could think of two people who could well control production and service, one of them the woman who was currently Clayton's second-in-command.

Hemmings was no problem, and in any event he was quite certain that if he left, Scott & Ballinger would quickly find a replacement.

Solving such problems, he mused, was one task that a managing director should not delegate. He should tackle the worst jobs, inspiring by example. Brennan even began to enjoy the thought of the challenge ahead; but that enjoyment didn't last long. Linklaters had to put things right fast, and to make money fast. The defection of managers, even one of them, would again shake employee confidence.

But Canada Copiers couldn't take on everyone. Cornell

was no fool, and he didn't throw away money; also he
had his own staff to consider.

He thought again of the alternatives. If one went, who
would it be? The obvious choice for Canada would be
Spurling, and Spurling did want a top job.

Spurling knew all about the plans for the future, knew
every aspect of manufacturing, knew whether the problems could be solved or not. Yes, he would be a valuable
prize!

But Spurling seemed so keen on the new quality
control plans. Could he be such a consummate actor?
And if it was Spurling, and he seemed the obvious
choice, the only other person he would want to take with
him would be Clayton.

If, on the other hand, it was Wallace – and he very
much doubted that – then Wallace might want to take
Strong along with him.

He continued turning these thoughts around in his
mind until he had a brilliant idea. Unwrapping himself
from the blankets, he left the top deck and made his way
to the cashier's office on 2 Deck. The assistant recognised
him and said politely, "Good morning Mr Brennan."

"Good morning," he answered. "I've just made a
decision and I want you to help me carry it out. As you
know, my associates use their individual credit facilities
and sign for all services. As this is a business trip, I feel I
should pay their bills regardless – the drinks in their
rooms, their telephone calls – I've decided that I should
meet these charges; so would you, therefore, arrange to
have all the bills they sign added to my account for
payment."

"That shouldn't be any trouble," said the assistant,
"I'll have to confirm it." He went away, returning shortly
to say, "That will be quite in order, Mr Brennan. Do you
want the accounts together with all the chits for checking, or do you wish your associates to check them?"

"No, leave it all to me, I don't want them bothered. If

they have had the odd drink or two, it doesn't matter very much. I'll be along on Friday to settle up with you."

"Thank you, sir."

When he arrived back in the meeting room, Hemmings said, "That was a good paper you wrote, Bob. We couldn't improve on it, only elaborate on some points."

"Good," said Brennan, then, "I have some news for you. I telephoned the office and spoke to Cathy. She had been trying to get through to me. Who do you think has approached her with a view to a job with us?"

They all made wild guesses, but none was right.

"None other," said Brennan, "than Canada Copiers' late personnel manager, Donald Powell. He'll certainly be worth talking to, whether we take him on or not!"

Brennan smiled at his managers and said, "Now let's go through all your elaborations and make a final decision about quality meetings, so that we have the basis for a chapter in our manual."

The discussion continued until lunchtime.

Later that day one of the managers telephoned Mark Cornell of Canada Copiers.

19 The team solves problems

Maybe it's my imagination, thought Brennan over lunch, *but some of the hilarity seems a little forced*. On his way back to the meeting he was, again, considering every alternative. He arrived at only one definite decision – until he knew for certain the names of the defectors, he would carry on as if nothing was amiss. On Friday the truth must emerge. The mole could not know if Donald Powell had learned of his boss's manipulations while he was still with Canada Copiers, and would want to discover quickly whether he – Brennan – was aware of what was taking place. Brennan also decided that the confrontation should take place in the London office on the following Monday morning, when he was determined to sack the culprit before any of the defectors could give him notice.

Straightening his shoulders, he entered the meeting room. The managers were in a huddle. What, he wondered, were they discussing? Casting aside his suspicions, and smiling as if nothing untoward had occurred, he said, "Let's get started."

The managers sat down, and Brennan continued, "In this session we are tackling problem-solving. First, we must decide the basic rules, then we can consider problems and their solutions as they apply to us as managers. So back to basics:

1. Define the problem. Too often there is an attempt to solve a subsidiary problem when the real problem has not been identified. Harvey, I know, will agree with me that when sales fall, the salesman will identify the problem as being due to either high prices or extreme competition. The sales manager may well identify the problem as being caused by the company falling behind technically, owing to the inefficiency of production or R&D. Someone else may consider the problem is due to poor service or lack of marketing skills. There may be subsidiary reasons, but the real problem could be simply a lack of effective sales management.

   Many sales managers, when sales fall, immediately side with the salesmen, and agree that prices are too high or competitors are undercutting. They will never admit the fact that they have become 'armchair sales managers' who no longer motivate their teams, and without continual motivation a sales force will always fail when the going gets tough.

   To discover the real problem is difficult. The sales manager presents a strong case to his managing director that prices are too high. If, however, he is a very good managing director, he will carry out the first step in problem-solving: *to determine the real problem.*

   After careful investigation he may identify the real problem, and will then move on to Step 2.

2. Accumulate all the information and facts that could have any bearing on the problem.

3. Interpret the information. This may lead to new thinking. It may be that the managing director will then decide that the real problem has not yet been identified, and he will go back to Step 1. When he has identified the real problem – that the sales manager is at fault for not motivating his team – he will move on to Step 4.

4. Find solutions to the problem.

5. With several solutions to consider, he will select the best practical solution, bearing in mind how the decision could affect the future. If he is satisfied that his decision is correct he will then move on to Step 6.

6. Test out his solutions, if that is at all possible. If it is not feasible, give the necessary instructions to ensure that his decision is implemented.

"These six steps make up the standard problem-solving formula, and work most of the time. There is also a short cut to problem-solving that is always worthy of consideration.

"First, look for the obvious solution. It is remarkable the number of times a mechanical fault, a breakdown, or a human relations problem is due to an obvious cause which is overlooked while the abstract is considered. If there is no obvious cause, go to the other extreme. Consider the most improbable solutions. The best way to achieve a result here is by means of a brain-storming session."

Brennan paused, took a deep breath, then continued, "Finally, remember the main problem with problem-solving: it is *people*. *People* take up a stance and won't budge. *People* become too emotionally involved. *People's* advice can be clouded by dislikes. *People* will only recognise a problem and consider a solution if someone else is to blame. *People* exaggerate. *People* suffer from stress, which makes them mislead others investigating the cause. In the workshop *people* blame their tools, when it is *people* who are at fault. Understand *people* and you are halfway towards solving almost any problem."

Once more Brennan paused and glanced at each of the managers in turn. He said, "So much for the generalities of problem-solving. What I am looking for now is examples of problem-solving as applied to managers rather than managing directors. Would you like to begin, Mike?"

Spurling said, "A good example of problem-solving applicable to manufcturing procedures would take hours, days, or weeks, and would bore everyone. But I can give you yet another formula that works more often than not.

"The six points you made, Bob, are valid, and apply to most forms of problem-solving, but what we look for in the production line when things go wrong is nonconformance. Whatever the standards, every aspect of manufacture must conform to something – a specification, a speed, a quantity, a timetable, a set order of events, checking. Every component must be made to a standard. Each weld must be on target, and there must be a standard evenness of paint spraying. Therefore, if a problem occurs, the first thing we look for is *nonconformance*. The aim is to discover what is different. Discover the *nonconformance* and you will find the cause of the problem.

"I would advise everyone concerned with problem-solving to consider the rule of non-conformance. It can apply with people, as well as machines. Someone acts out of character – he is *nonconforming*. Why? No sleep, troubles at home, too much to drink, ill health . . . Could that person be the cause of a problem? Could the problem be averted by the company appreciating what is happening to that person? Why has someone suddenly changed a viewpoint that he has held for a long time? Why does that sound, solid, supervisor suddenly step out of line?

"Look for *nonconformance* of *people* and you will not have to go through the six steps to solve the problem."

"That's excellent!" Brennan said, amidst general applause for Mike's contribution, then, "How about you now, Harvey?"

"Thanks boss, but you've already stolen my best story. I was all set to tell a spellbinding tale of how weak sales management can cause more problems than competitors – but you got in first!"

"Sorry, Harvey, maybe it was you told it to me in the first place. But I'm sure you can think of another example."

Harvey thought for a few moments, then said, "A heavy cost is that of producing brochures, leaflets, explanatory booklets, etc. It's a real problem to keep this cost down. The very best salesmen don't distribute leaflets in the vain hope that they will bring in some business, but the average salesman – and he makes up 80 per cent of every sales force – is always a leaflet-dropper.

"That is the problem identified. Unfortunately, few salesmen can put themselves in the place of a buyer. What they fail to realise is that when sales leaflets are left for later consideration, probably 90 per cent of them are thrown straight into the waste paper basket as the salesman leaves. Nine per cent suffer the same fate a day or so later, and the 1 per cent that are filed for future reference are generally soon forgotten.

"There are, of course, exceptions. Engineering data technicalities can be stored for consideration at a later date, but they are not sales literature. Sales leaflets are something different. These are mainly for the use of the salesman, to enable him to explain his offer fully and in a logical sequence – and that is mostly their only use. Sales literature is only read avidly by those who *want* to buy something, for example, anything relating to a hobby. Such literature is read line by line. But that is because of our keenness for our likely purchase.

"Professional buyers, however, rarely study any sales literature carefully. For all the hours spent on direct mail sales literature, it never seems to dawn on the leaflet droppers that the request 'leave me a leaflet' is only a ploy to get rid of the salesman."

Brennan interrupted, "I don't want to cut you short, Harvey, but you do have a complete session to follow.

This session is on problem-solving."

The Strong beard jutted for a moment, then Harvey decided not to make an issue of it. He said, "I agree, Bob, but I have the solution to this problem, and it applies to many similar problems as well. Pleading is a waste of time because the droppers are always sure they are right. Controlling by giving minimal supplies never works, because the droppers will always find some means of getting hold of extra leaflets. The real problem is weak salesmanship on the part of weak salesmen, who salve their consciences by believing they are selling when they give away leaflets.

"The way to solve this problem is *publicity*, and publicity can solve many problems.

"When it happened to me in my previous company, I gave the sales force the facts about costs – that costs were getting out of hand and costs had to be reduced. One factor in these costs was increased expenditure on sales literature. I told them that for the next six months in the weekly bulletin I would be giving details of the sales figures of each salesman, together with the sales costs, and the relation between sales and costs. The costs would be broken down so that the salesmen who used their car too frequently would know that they, too, were wasting the company's money and time, and the leaflet dropper would see how much his habit was costing the company.

"Even the least sensitive of salesmen, if he knew his costs were too high, might consider that his days with the company were likely to be very limited unless he took action.

"Too many companies seem afraid to tell the members of their staff the exact cost that each of them incurs in the performance of his duties."

"Well done," said Brennan, "it's a little adrift from the ordinary managerial problem, but it is a good lesson. I agree, too many managers are cagey about the profits and costs. They shouldn't be."

It was at this stage that Brennan decided that Harvey Strong was not one of the possible defectors.

"Now over to you, Laurie."

Wallace wanted to impress his colleagues, and had carefully worked out in his mind an excellent formula for solving problems. He began, "We managers – I presume we are looked upon as middle managers – probably handle more problems in a day than the Board has to consider in a month. The Board is concerned with big but occasional problems – the problem of overseas losses, the problem of a possible merger, the problem of dissatisfied shareholders, the problem of investment, the problem of strategy – but we have daily problems, which, if not dealt with immediately, can turn into big problems that might then have to be dealt with at board level. The harmony of the business depends so much on us, the middle managers. Managers with particular functions have problems associated with those functions – witness the excellent contributions by our friends Harvey and Mike. But a general manager – and no one has adequately defined the job specification of a general manager, except to say that he generally manages – is mostly concerned with people.

"There are awkward people, and their awkwardness causes problems. There are people who always believe they are right, and they, too, cause problems. There are people who complain, people who get ulcers from not complaining, people who will stab you in the back while smiling to your face – that's probably impossible but I'm sure you understand the metaphor – people who won't share their office, people who want a particular kind of office, people who are overworked, people who are underworked. They all cause problems. There are the people who arrive late, causing others to say, 'Why should we be early if he's always allowed to come late?' – another problem. People have opinions as to what should be done about everything, and they express these opinions among themselves, causing discontent perhaps, and more problems.

"This is everyday life. This is what happens in families, in villages, in towns . . . What does a manager do when A insists that he will not allow a certain action to be taken? 'Over my dead body!' he will say. What happens when B feels he is entitled to this or that, and management has opposite views?

"I have found the ideal way to solve most of these problems. It is based on the fact that when we think of something ourselves – as has already been mentioned – we readily agree to anything suggested on similar lines to our own thoughts, while we are opposed to most suggestions coming from other people. All we have to remember, therefore, are what I term *the magic words*. These are:

"You mentioned to me the other day . . .
"I remember when you told me . . .
"You will recall that you first put forward the idea some months ago . . .
"I have thought very carefully about the point you raised . . .

"White lies? Possibly! But white lies can be perfectly acceptable. They don't harm anyone. All that happens is that we are suggesting to Mr A or Mr B that they thought of something first. They will rarely admit to forgetfulness. It is, again, a fact that we all like to believe our advice has been accepted. I can assure you, gentlemen, the system works. You don't need to do it all the time, only now and again, when someone seems quite intractable."

Spurling said, "From now on I shall never again believe I ever suggested anything to you."

Laughter again erupted around the room, and Brennan could hardly believe that one or possibly two defectors were taking part in such an enjoyable session.

They spent some time discussing the various implications of problem-solving, and then Brennan said, "Now it's your turn, Victor."

Clayton said, "The main problem area in many companies is handling complaints so that customer goodwill is maintained, because customers always think they are right. Many of the chief executives of highly efficient companies visit their factories, stores, or distribution centres regularly, and talk to as many employees as possible – an excellent form of human relations – but they never get a true picture of what happens behind the scenes. However, that is not their objective. Their objective is, in the main, to create goodwill. The truth about the effectiveness of a company can sometimes only be learned by a deep investigation into what is now euphemistically called a 'customer relations division'. In smaller companies such as ours complaints go direct to the various divisions in the organisation, and service gets most of them. When a chief executive visits the customer relations division, he is met by cover-ups.

"If anyone takes the trouble to write to the managing director of a large company, it is highly doubtful whether he ever sees that letter. His secretary passes it on to the customer relations division, so that the chief executive thinks all is well when it need not, necessarily, be so.

"Earlier, you, Laurie, told the story of how one world-famous company employed a sales manager who was totally inefficient. Would a visiting managing director learn of his inefficiency just by talking to him? Would he ever find out that enquiries were not being dealt with adequately?

"Doubtful! Yet here we have one of our most important problems, the problem of satisfying customers – maybe small customers who will one day become very big customers if their goodwill is retained.

"I wonder if any chief executive has ever tried to get service from his own company. Let him try telephoning for service. Almost certainly he will find the lines engaged, and he will have to make anything from three to six attempts before he gets through. Is that good service? How many frustrated customers have said, 'That's the last time I buy anything from them'?

"Is it that the bosses don't want to know anything about weak service? Would they rather make the claim that they care for their customers, because they believe they do care for them, although lower down the scale there is no caring for customers at all? More problems!

"Has there ever been a service manager who didn't think the customer was wrong most of the time? More problems!

"These meetings are all about quality, Bob, and I've made up my mind that from now on service must improve its quality. In so many service departments you will hear the manager saying to someone, 'Tell him I'm out', 'Tell him I won't be back for two weeks', 'Tell him the engineer's on the way'.

"That manager doesn't have the guts to speak to his customers. Yet the solution is simple: all those in a company concerned with handling complaints must be trained, and should subsequently attend refresher courses, on *How to win over customers who believe they are right when, in fact, they are wrong*. In too many companies the wrong people are in a position to do a great deal of damage to the good name of that company. My plea is for all chief executives – and if I may say so, that includes you, Bob – to hold regular reviews of complaint procedures, and to make regular tests to ensure that complaints are being dealt with adequately. That way, many of the problems will be solved."

Clayton's contribution led to a great deal of argument, – especially from Laurie Wallace, who felt that as general manager he was already occupied in the handling of complaints. Clayton forbore from telling him that he was one of those people who would call out, 'Tell him I'm away'.

Brennan looked at his watch. "It's lunch time," he said. "We'll have your thoughts after lunch, Richard."

When they returned from lunch, Hemmings began, "As I have mentioned previously, an accountant should never discuss his work in general terms – there could be repercussions. However, I will mention one problem affecting every company of every size, and that is the expense account. It is a problem because once it gets out of hand, no one seems to have the strength of character to control it. All those who receive expenses seem to look on them not as repayments for cash laid out but rather as extra perks. I can't agree that that is an ethical way of thinking. To me there are always parameters of expenses that should not be exceeded; if they are exceeded, there are always problems, especially when employees believe that they are working extremely hard for the benefit of the company, and cannot see why they should be criticised for spending money needlessly.

"It is always my duty to bring to the notice of the manager concerned that there are overpayments to staff in his division. This sort of occurrence rarely reaches the managing director's ears. Why should it? He should not have to attend to such day to day matters; it is up to the manager to put things right. Unfortunately, however, all too often it is the managers who are the worst offenders, so they can hardly criticise members of their staff for behaving in a similar manner. But no managing director, if it comes to his ears, is ever misled by the manipulation of staff expenses, and neither is any good accountant. We all know of the person who seems to manage to fit his holidays in with that special business trip overseas. Who does he think he is misleading? But, of course, there can be no proof that he has really taken part of his holiday at the company's expense.

"Should anything be done about this? Most certainly! If not, others will take the same steps.

"In some organisations it is the standard perk for many salesmen to ensure that every member of their family uses petrol at the company's expense. Everyone knows how this can be achieved. No manager should ever be misled on this score.

"If records are kept, and records are checked, it will soon become obvious that a lot of unnecessary mileage is being claimed.

"I won't go into this in any further detail, but it is wide-ranging, and the answer is simple: from the very moment someone is engaged it should be made very clear that there is always a tight rein kept on expenses. Everyone must be aware that an expense sheet is scrutinised very carefully. Remember, once anyone has got away with a pound, next time it will be two pounds. When large expense claims are made and passed, it is always the fault of a manager. And when this happens in the case of managers, it is always the fault of the managing director.

"If we want quality in an organisation, the salary scale should be high – as Bob has promised it will be in our group – so that there will be no need for anyone to try and obtain that extra perk. If a manager is afraid of upsetting a member of his staff by querying an expense account, that manager should resign."

Hemmings stopped talking, and Brennan clapped, though no one else did. Possibly they all felt a little guilty, thought Brennan, but he said, "I'll make no comment on that – it is a good contribution, about an issue that is rarely faced up to." Then he went on, "And now I should like to make a final point.

"So many problems at middle management level are not solved because those concerned believe in 'management by *not* looking'. The obvious example, as we have all seen on occasion, is when a diner in a restaurant complains to a waiter, and the manager disappears into the kitchen. Management by *not looking* is very prevalent, but it is not the way to solve problems, so let us be sure that we, as quality managers, take control immediately we realise that a problem has arisen. We must set the example."

. Tea was brought in by a steward. While the cups were being poured, Brennan said, "We might have an early evening if Harvey doesn't keep us too long for the final session."

"Is that a command?" asked Strong.

20   An interlude

Brennan had arranged to meet Vivienne about four o'clock. He needed someone to talk to, and Vivienne was a wonderful listener.

When he walked into the cabin, Vivienne was sitting in a chair reading the entertainment leaflet. She said immediately, "I do hope you're not going to finish late, we have to be at the party at seven-fifteen."

"What party?"

Vivienne explained. Everything had happened so quickly that Brennan had forgotten that he, Viv, and the team, had been invited that evening to the captain's quarters for cocktails.

Brennan said, "I had forgotten, but everything is under control. I told Harvey not to take too long over the final session. We should be free by six, which should give us plenty of time to relax and change."

"How did you manage to get through the session," Vivienne asked, "without them noticing that you're not your usual, happy self?"

"I managed. Incidentally, I've ruled out Harvey and also Richard. That leaves Laurie, Mike, or Victor, and of the three I think it must be Mike. He's the one man Cornell would like to get hold of. But I shall know by tomorrow evening, so let's not worry."

"But you are worrying."

"Not at all! I've told you before, problem-solving is not worrying. Worrying is when a task is beyond you, and you can't confide your problem to anyone who could get you off the hook. I'm problem-solving not worrying. What news have you got?"

"Penny fell over and hurt her ankle. She went to the doctor, who is evidently so tall and handsome that she immediately ignored his advice that there was nothing seriously wrong and only cold water compresses were needed, and made another appointment for later this evening. You wouldn't have thought that of Penny, would you?"

"Why not? I shouldn't be surprised if the next thing we hear is that Tina has gone to visit the doctor as well."

"I doubt it! Incidentally, Tina won the scrabble contest. Mary is taken up with astronomy and is attending lectures, but I haven't seen anything of Pat or Dorothy." Then, switching the subject, she asked, "What will you do when you know the identity of the mole?"

"Nothing, while we're still on the QE2. I'll take 'em all by surprise when we meet on Monday."

21 Every manager is a sales manager

Brennan began the final session of the day by saying, "At our first meeting in London – it seems years ago, doesn't it? – I told you that we were going to knock hell out of our competitors by being better managers, by making quality an obsession, and, equally important, by outselling them.

"Why am I so confident of victory? Because, in the main, salesmanship worldwide is poor to average. The exceptions are those companies whose chief executives know that when all other things are equal – when their competitors can spend as much on advertising as *they* can, when their competitors can spend as much on promotion as *they* can, when their competitors' technologists are just about as good as are their own – orders will go to those who employ the most highly skilled and respected salesmen.

"Most companies' chief executives are accountants, engineers, scientists, bankers – rarely marketing men. A non-sales-minded executive can obviously be an outstanding manager, but unfortunately some still believe that, because of the technical or price advantage of their product, buyers will queue up at their door.

"They won't! Usually, owing to the size and wealth of some of our great enterprises, they will hold their share of the market. But that is all. If a managing director is satisfied just to hold his share of the market, he should resign. Because they believe they are more efficient than

174

their competitors, brilliant managers want more than their allotted share.

"We must win, if every one of our managers becomes a part-time sales manager. What do I mean by that?

"Who is at fault when an enquiry is not dealt with immediately? A manager.

"Who is at fault when no one checks to discover if an enquiry sent to a salesman has been followed up? A manager.

"Who is at fault when a good customer is alienated by receipt of an 'unless' letter sent by mistake? A manager.

"Who is to blame when a salesman becomes dispirited because a commission cheque is late arriving, or there has been an incorrect deduction? A manager.

"Who is to blame if a salesman does not sell well after receiving a letter severely reprimanding him, when a friendly telephone call could have resolved the issue? A manager.

"Who is at fault when a switchboard operator, a clerk or an assistant doesn't know how to speak correctly on the telephone? A manager.

"Now I hope you get my point, that *all* managers should be part-time sales managers. Managers in every department can often make or mar a sale.

"There are some managers who not only do not help a salesman, but actually hinder him.

"Why? Because salesmen aren't popular if they nag, persevere, make demands, for what they believe to be right. These attitudes antagonise managers who have no concept of what selling entails. They don't realise that if a salesman is not capable of nagging, demanding, persevering, for what he believes to be right, he will never be a good salesman.

"Just one more point: technical men are sent out by technical managers, who believe that all a prospective buyer wants to hear is technicalities. These managers forget, because they don't understand selling, that all the

buyers want to hear is how the technicalities will benefit
them.

"Again, who is at fault? Why, the technical manager,
who has no idea of what salesmanship means . . ."

"Hold on," interrupted Strong, "you're poaching right
on to my territory! You told me that your introduction
would only be to show how every manager can influence
sales. Now you're getting down to the nitty-gritty of
selling."

Brennan laughed. "You're quite right, Harvey – sorry!
It's all yours now."

Strong stood up. "I always think more clearly when
I'm on my feet," he said.

"You mean it puts you in a superior position," said
Wallace.

"That too!" rejoined Strong, then went on quickly,
"Bob has explained that a company is only sales-minded
when all the managers realise that their jobs, as well as
those of all the other employees, depend so much on
whether or not the product sells in the market place.
Very often when companies go bust, it is because no one
has listened to the salesman – he is considered a bloody
nuisance if he persists in saying that something is not
quite right with the product or service. But it is the
salesman who knows when a product is the wrong shape,
size, or colour. And if the salesman does complain, what
happens? No one will agree with him. The managing
director may even tell the sales manager to *'tell him to get
up off his backside and go out and sell'.*

"Most managing directors side with their indoor teams
because the indoor teams are able to present to them only
one side of the picture. In any event, no managing
director likes to think that there could conceivably be
anything wrong with *his* company or *his* products.

"To repeat what has been said earlier, what is the use
of a chef claiming that his food is perfect when the
customer is railing at the waiter for serving him shoe

leather covered in a gooey sauce? It is only the waiter who knows the truth, because he hears it from the customer."

Strong almost glared at each of the managers in turn, as if they were guilty, and said, "When you sell, you learn the truth, don't you?"

"But we don't sell anything," said Spurling.

"Of course you do!" answered Strong. "What is the salesman's main purpose when he makes the call? Surely it is to influence a mind – allied, of course, to satisfying the customer's needs. You, Mike, are a member of your local Conservative Party Committee, and at the last election you canvassed on behalf of your candidate. If, when contacting a householder, you were told that he was a staunch Conservative, there would have been no mind to influence, just a handshake and 'Goodbye'. But if your next call was on an SDP or Labour supporter, you would be met by an immediate objection. You could, then, either walk away – and you wouldn't think much of a salesman who walked away when his customer objected to making a purchase – or you would stay on and try to influence the mind of the voter. You would do this by answering the objections he raised, and then stressing to him all the benefits to the local community and to the country if the Conservative party were in power.

"Now that, Mike, is 80 per cent salesmanship. So you will see that you are a salesman, because you do try, on occasion, to influence minds."

Spurling smiled, but did not contradict Harvey's statement.

Strong turned to Clayton and said, "And you, Victor, told me that when you were buying your new house, you approached your bank for a personal loan. How did you go about that?

"First, knowing you, you meticulously prepared your case, and that is probably 10 per cent of selling. Then, before your meeting, you would have rehearsed in your mind the order in which you would put forward your proposal.

"You told me your bank manager quoted you too high a rate. You then tried to influence his mind to give you better terms.

"So, Victor, you must agree that there are many occasions on which you, too, are a salesman doing your best to *influence minds*.

"Why, then, do so many people who spend much of their time selling their ideas to others belittle salesmanship? It is because they form a false judgement by watching so-called salesmen in action on TV, or reading about disreputable salesmen in newspapers or novels.

"Let me, therefore, give you a better understanding of salesmanship, because, as Bob said, your future participation in our selling effort is essential to our success.

"Firstly, there is a continual appraisal of a salesman's work. If certain levels of achievement are not met, the salesman can be faced with dismissal. This hardly applies to any other walk of business life. For an office worker it may take years, if ever, before it becomes generally known that he is inefficient; there is so much covering up that can be done in an office or factory. But there is no cover-up for a salesman. There's nowhere for him to hide.

"In the field of selling everyone lives by results, and these results are scrutinised right up to managing director level. No salesman can mislead others as to his brilliance. Sales figures tell all!

"Because it is axiomatic of life that we dislike people who bore us, are antagonised by someone's dress or manner, have little time for those who are for ever telling us their troubles, we sometimes have no alternative but to get along with such people, possibly associates, as best we can. But buyers do have alternatives. They need not grant interviews, spare much time, or place orders with those who may annoy or depress them. Therefore, salesmen suffering from migraine, colds, the after-effects of a family row, rising blood pressure at not being able to park a car, etc. must still, when making a call, appear bright and enthusiastic. And that takes some doing, day after day. If management understood what salesmen are up against in the field, I'm quite sure there would be more co-operation and friendliness – and willingness, too, to help, in spite of a salesman's temporary lack of tact or loss of temper."

Wallace said, "Oh, we're not as bad as all that!"

"I don't think you are, Laurie, I'm generalising."

Wallace said, "Thank you, Harvey. I'm glad you agree that some of your high-pressure boys can be more than difficult, and we all have our limits of patience."

Strong said, "We haven't any so-called high-pressure boys. If we had, they wouldn't sell if we gave 50 per cent discount. Professional buyers strongly object to being pressurised."

This time it was Hemmings' turn to interrupt. He said, "I saw a TV documentary recently about some poor old boy who had been nagged by a salesman into buying shares he didn't want and, consequently, lost money."

"Richard, that's just the cue I wanted! There are con men in every walk of life – shady solicitors, drug-peddling doctors, unfrocked men of the Church, and crooked politicians – but they are a tiny minority. There is no news value in the 99 per cent of church leaders who do their best, each week, to lead us to a better life; and there is certainly no news value in the solicitor honestly advising his clients to the best of his ability. To show on TV a salesman carrying out his daily task diligently with the objective of satisfying his customer needs would cause instant switch-off. High pressure, then, which means pressuring people to buy, only applies to a few salesmen who use these tactics on householders. They couldn't use them on professional buyers. Have I killed the high-pressure canard?"

"Yes," said Spurling with a smile. "But only because we are getting near to drinking time! Joking aside, though, you've made your point so far as I'm concerned."

Hemmings said, "I agree. You've made your point with me, too. Obviously, I've never given enough thought to the sales side of the business."

"You're excused," said Strong, "I haven't given much thought to the financial side, but I mean to put that right."

Spurling said, "There is one point I would like to raise; you expressed the view that salesmanship generally is not perhaps quite as good as it should be. How about our team? Do you consider them good, bad, or indifferent?"

"They're good – damned good! They prove the point that sometimes, even if things are unequal, the brilliant salesman will still often beat the poor salesman in spite of the latter's advantages, say, in price or design. However, there are two or three in the team who will have to do better if they want to stay with us. The changes that Bob has suggested, concentrating on certain areas, won't worry our top men at all. We still have a bloody good product – the best on the market, in my opinion. Our problems all stemmed from the extras that went wrong."

Bob Brennan was very pleased with the way the session was going. He could sense that Harvey was winning the managers over.

Wallace said, "What part does marketing play? You're expressing only one aspect of marketing, and that is selling. It seems to me that in your view that is the all-important factor."

"No, I'm not making that claim. Only that it is a very great factor in the successful company, and that sometimes it is not given its proper place in the marketing plan. Bob knows our marketing strategies will also have to be overhauled. Salesmen can't win in isolation. Marketing covers advertising, promotions, pricing policies, strategies, and I'm not claiming that a salesman can survive without that backing; but neither can all the marketing skills in the world take the place of the crunch meeting. That is between salesman and buyer."

Wallace said, "If you are right, why isn't more attention paid to the selling effort? After all, we have some highly skilled professional marketing managers in this country."

"Fair enough! I think the problem arose because when the true potential of marketing was realised some years back, the sales manager often became the marketing manager – it was only a change of title. He, in turn, promoted someone from the office, or a field manager, to take his place as sales manager. This led to the downgrading of sales management. With the arrival of professional marketing managers this is gradually being overcome.

"You asked me the question why some companies don't give priority to selling. The reason possibly is that it takes time for sales management to be upgraded, so that it is only just below Board level."

Strong looked at his watch. "I don't think I need continue. All I've attempted to do is to convince you that all managers should be sales-minded if salesmen are to get the backing that must lead to a higher turnover."

Bob said, "Well done, Harvey. You've made out a splendid case. Let me assure you that my aim is for us to become the most sales-orientated company in the copier field."

There was applause for Harvey Strong. Then Brennan said, "Tomorrow the final session will cover delegation, to be followed by motivation.

"I have already discussed the delegating section with Laurie, who, having made a study of the subject, will open the session. Because of the time factor I have asked him to enumerate only the main points." He paused, then went on, "That's all for today. Remember, at seven-fifteen we are all due at the captain's quarters for his cocktail party, and later there is going to be a gala dinner in the Queen's room. As agreed earlier, we have all 'done our own thing' up till now and that, I am sure, has helped to make the crossing so enjoyable for everyone. Wives don't want to have to listen to business talk all the time. But I think it would be rather nice if we all celebrated the end of our sessions and the near conclusion of our voyage, together. Brian and Jill Moss will also join us. How do you feel about that?"

Everyone wholeheartedly agreed, and the managers trooped out.

Brennan thought none of them looked anything but keenly enthusiastic. He sighed deeply, and followed them.

22 Motivation

The previous evening had been a great success. After watching the all-star cabaret show, they had danced at the Lido Night Club, followed by gambling at the Casino.

In the bedroom, just after two am, Bob had said to Vivienne, "It was a great get-together, wasn't it? The biggest mystery to me is which one of them is acting a part."

At nine am all but one of the slightly bleary-eyed managers were looking forward to an afternoon's sleep, before packing. The luggage had to be ready for collection by six o'clock. The one exception to the red-eyed brigade was Laurie Wallace.

Trim, smart, as alert as ever, he looked as though he had spent the previous evening drinking Perrier water. Everyone agreed that he was the great imbiber.

There was no introduction from Brennan, and Wallace began, "My friends, this is my last opportunity to hold you entranced."

This led immediately to a series of jocular remarks.

"I'll start again," said Wallace. "I was looking forward to holding you entranced by my exposition on the art of delegation, but Bob has decided that after last night I should now be even briefer than had been my original intention. In short, Bob said, 'Just give 'em the facts!'

"So be it! First, I must emphasise that delegating is

one of the strongest of all motivational forces. Even anti-everything people change for the better when asked by a manager to undertake some special task for him. Delegating, then, means handing over responsibility, and responsibility motivates subordinates to give of their best. Here are the main factors which apply to delegating:

1. It saves a manager's time and allows him to concentrate on more important matters.
2. It gives a manager more *thinking* time, rather than *acting* time.
3. How else can one assess a subordinate's ability to undertake specific tasks, other than by giving him such tasks to complete?
4. To *do* is the best form of learning, and training. Therefore, by *delegating*, subordinates are also being trained to improve their abilities and skills.
5. Subordinates are made to feel that they are contributing to the management function.
6. It bulds a subordinate's ego, and we all need ego-building on occasion.
7. If a manager is promoted, he will more rapidly be able to name a successor if that person has already carried out several tasks delegated to him."

Wallace paused, then continued, "Is that snappy enough, Bob?"

"No," answered Brennan with a smile. "You can reduce it still more."

"Very well! On to some delegating rules:

1. Begin by delegating simple tasks.
2. Do not delegate to sensitive individuals, to whom even the simplest tasks are a strain.
3. Don't allow those you delegate to delegate to others in their turn, unless they have your permission.
4. Always explain the full purpose of an assignment, and

spell out not only the objective, but, if possible, how that objective is likely to benefit the subordinate, the manager, or the company.

5. Always explain the parameters of authority, otherwise conflict with others could arise.
6. Although authority has been given to carry out a task, the task should always be monitored.
7. If a task is not completed satisfactorily, do not criticise strongly, but try to draw a lesson from what has happened so that the subordinate may benefit from his mistakes. If the task has been completed satisfactorily, give credit and praise."

Wallace paused, to sip some water and to ask if there were any questions. There were none, so he continued, "Let us now consider some other aspects of delegation:

1. Possibly a subordinate will not carry out a task as efficiently as would the manager himself – not in the early days anyway. If there is any doubt about the subordinate's ability, the manager should monitor the task closely, so that his advice and guidance can lead to the subordinate's success, and instil in him confidence in his future.
2. The manager who over-delegates may lose touch with events.
3. Not everyone is capable of accepting responsibility. The manager must take care, therefore, not to delegate to the wrong people just because he wants to get rid of an onerous task.
4. Because a subordinate is not up to a manager's standard of efficiency, a target should be set to give the subordinate ample time to complete the assignment, and the subordinate should agree to the time schedule.
5. If a subordinate makes a mistake, the manager may be reprimanded. That's fair enough! However, it should not stop the manager delegating."

Before Wallace could continue, Strong said, "What are we all going to do with our time when we delegate and delegate – and delegate again?"

Brennan answered, before Wallace could reply. "Don't worry about that, Harvey, I'll always make sure you never have time to put your feet up on the desk and study the racing results."

Light-hearted banter continued for a few minutes, then Wallace shouted, "Order, order!"

When quiet was restored, Wallace said "We're wasting time, and that is against Bob's orders. Now let us start thinking of some of the barriers to delegating. While some managers think it is right to delegate, many more think it is right for the *other* managers but not for them. Why is this?

"Here are some of the reasons:

1. If a manager has a grasshopper mind – if his office has all the appearance of a secondhand bookshop, if he has no idea of time management – he will never be sufficiently well organised to delegate.
2. If a manager is intolerant, impatient, and never believes that subordinates are as efficient, or keen, as he was when he was a youngster, he will mislead himself into believing that he can always do the job more quickly and better than anyone else.
3. Another manager will claim, possibly with some truth, 'I have no one to delegate to.' These days it is rare for a department to be overstaffed, and this can result in all-round pressure. The answer is a staff training programme that includes time management. Pressure is often caused by lack of understanding of what time management implies. It applies as much to a typist, a computer operator, a technician, or an engineer, as it does to a cashier.
4. This doesn't apply to anyone here, but it is worth bearing in mind. If a manager feels insecure, he will

be loath to delegate in case the subordinate's ability is noticed to his – the manager's – detriment. That is why an insecure manager never has a highly competent staff and – yes – their incompetence is a reason for not delegating.

5. Forgetfulness is a barrier to delegating. The busy manager becomes so immersed in his work that he forgets that it is his duty to delegate whenever possible.

6. A manager may not want to test his theory that no one else can do the work as well as he, because it may be proved wrong.

7. A manager may want to create the image of a dynamic go-getter, by always having a full 'in' tray, by continual use of the telephone and an engaged signal switched on, more often than not, outside his office door. This manager is usually on a personal ego-trip, and delegating would result in his bluff being called. He is not really as busy as he makes himself out to be."

Wallace thought for a few seconds, looked around the room and said, "Can anyone think of any other barriers to delegation?"

No one made any comment, so Wallace went on, "A most important point is that we are all apt to delegate the unpleasant tasks. That isn't fair! These are the tasks which we managers should tackle ourselves. For example, speaking over the telephone to irate customers, reprimanding someone, telling staff about economies which have to be made . . ."

Spurling interrupted, "How about this one? A supervisor is delegated the authority to reprimand a worker for absenteeism, for example, or because of bad working habits. If the reprimand has little effect, the supervisor has to bring the culprit to the manager to be disciplined. What, though, if the manager finds that the culprit has, in fact, been abiding by the company rules? Does he back the supervisor in spite of this or, in all fairness, does he take the part of the worker?"

Wallace said, "Mike, you know the answer to that as well as I do. I think you are referring to a particular incident you had. The manager is at fault for not training the supervisor properly, so that he – the supervisor – knows that you can't reprimand a worker if he misuses the rules but doesn't break them. For example, the worker stays away, citing illness, but the supervisor suspects him of malingering. He can't be reprimanded unless there is proof of misconduct. Therefore, in this case, unfortunately, the manager must take the worker's side. But he should do so in such a way as not to embarrass the supervisor. And this should be followed by a long training session with the supervisor, so that he will never again put the manager in this difficult position. OK, Mike?"

"Fair enough!" said Spurling with a smile.

"One more point," said Wallace. "Don't forget that if a task is urgent, always try to give it to someone who has a sense of urgency, while the more routine tasks should be given to those who are more routine-minded.

"Now you will be glad to hear that I've reached the final points, *how to delegate:*

1. Explain the task *exactly*. The objective of the exercise and the actual results must be as clear to your subordinate as they are to you.
2. Clarify constraints and resources – time deadlines, expenditure, security considerations, etc.
3. Confirm briefly all aspects of the task, in writing, unless there is no scope at all for misunderstanding or later disagreement.
4. Explain the necessary training, advice, back-up, and support available.

5. Set up a review schedule so that you can check progress."

Wallace looked around. "Never fear, gentlemen," he said, "I have learned my lesson. Brevity is my keynote from now on. I'm about to finish. Remember to make sure that you are not delegating responsibility without also delegating authority to match. Do not give someone responsibility for certain activities if they do not have the necessary formal authority to control and influence the situation.

"Remember also that delegation is an *attitude of mind*, which has to be developed. Don't think, 'I'll do it myself unless there is a strong case for delegation'. Rather, act on the assumption that you can delegate, unless there is a cast-iron case for not doing so.

"Managers are in business to get results, and most managers are finally judged by their ability to motivate their subordinates. As I stated at the opening of this session, delegating is a great motivator.

"And that, I think you will agree, Bob, is the perfect lead in to your session."

Wallace beamed at his associates, and sat down.

Joining in the applause for Wallace, Brennan said, "Congratulations, Laurie, on covering all the aspects of delegation so succinctly. Now I'll try to emulate you."

He paused for effect, then went on, "As Laurie rightly pointed out, responsibility is one of the strongest of motivators. This, you will remember, was stressed earlier in our session on Quality Circles. In fact this may surprise you, but I believe responsibility is as strong a motivator as bonuses or incentives."

The managers did not agree with this assertion, although none of them expressed his views.

"At this stage," Brennan continued, "I do not expect any of you to credit this, but I shall make the point again, later. Firstly, let me have your views on how you motivate your teams to try just that little bit harder. You first, Mike."

Spurling said, "That's a difficult question. Let me tell you why.

"In nearly every work force throughout the country there are militants. By this I don't necesarily mean Marxists, Trotskyites, and the Militant Tendency nut cases, I am also referring to the men or women with a chip on their shoulder. Then there are those who can't credit that management could possibly have any good intentions, whatever they do. There is the 'Picker' – he picks at everything. The lights are too bright or not bright enough. In any case they are affecting his eyesight. The tea is too strong or too weak. The production line is too fast or too slow . . .

"When you consider that all companies employ some of these militants or semi-militants, you can see the problem I face in motivating the work force. The militant is always able to motivate his associates far more effectively than can any manager. He need not be a rabble-rouser, he need not even be popular, but when he says, 'They're having us on', 'Look at the profits they make', or 'They want us to . . .' he will always get nods of agreement. Nine times out of ten there is no following strike action, but there is a temporarily disgruntled work force, which can lead to a fall in output. In our case this happens rarely, but it does happen.

"In spite of these problems it is my job to motivate the workforce to maintain production and, on occasion, to pull out all the stops to meet a deadline.

"How do I achieve this aim?" Spurling paused, and everyone looked expectantly at him.

"I attended a course a year or so ago called *Situation Adaptable Leadership*. The instructor set out to prove that under present-day conditions there is no longer one effective leadership style. All leaders have to adapt to situations. I believe this also applies to managers, and motivation. What works one day may not have any effect the next, so I adjust my motivational style to suit the situation. Sometimes toughness is needed, but not often. Sometimes a cosy chat will bring the results. Sometimes a pat on the back, sometimes a man-to-man talk achieves the objective. I have found that there are very few long-term motivators; but there are many short-term motivators. This applies to production incentives, but it doesn't apply to pay rises, because, as Bob says, no worker's claim is ever met in full, and, therefore, he is never really satisfied with the awards.

"But back to situation-adaptable motivation. I very often use information as a motivator. It's surprising how workers react after hearing the truth about export sales, home sales, profit margins . . . But, in the main, I believe I motivate best by being completely honest and fair with all the work force, all the year round. I never lie to them. If they have a just case, as Richard knows, I'll put my job on the line for them. I never criticise one worker to another, and that is often a management weakness. I believe the determination on my part to be fair means that when a trouble-maker of one kind or another begins a campaign against management, the majority of the work force will not quite so readily accept the criticism. If the majority sees the manager as being fair, not sometimes not just on some days, but all the time, he will build a respect which even the most militant of left-wing workers will have difficulty in undermining.

"That, then, is my long-term motivator. We can use all kinds of gimmicks for short-term motivators. None of them compared with winning the respect of the work force."

As had become the practice, there was long applause for the contribution from Spurling.

Brennan said, "Your turn, Victor."

Clayton began, "My problem is not the same as Mike's. My problem is how to motivate engineers to maintain a good appearance, to create goodwill and to complete each job satisfactorily and tidily, when there is no direct control.

"Mike can see what goes on in the works every day. I can't see what happens on a customer's premises, so I use pride and competitiveness as motivators.

"About twice a year after a service call we send a request to the customer for information. It's the same sort of form as those we receive on this ship – as you know, there's a form in every cabin asking for passengers' views on the stewards, the food, hygiene, general service, etc. We list various items on our forms and ask for them to be marked from one to ten – one being poor, ten excellent. This, of course, covers appearance, performance, skills, tidiness, etc.

"Every six months there are special awards based on the response received to our questionnaires. But it isn't the rewards which really motivate, in my opinion, although they must have some effect in the short term. What motivates is the competitive spirit engendered. Every man wants to be featured in our prize award lists in the engineers' bulletins, where we print their photographs.

"So, as motivators, I find it is pride in achievement plus a competitive spirit that motivates engineers to give a little better than their best.

"And that is my contribution."

Again applause, and Brennan said, "Well done! So far we have as motivators *responsibility through delegation, situation-adaptable leadership, honesty and fair-mindedness, pride and competitiveness,* and *short-term incentives.* We have to practise what we preach, and remember them. Many managers read, listen, and learn; then they forget the basics of motivation."

He turned to Hemmings and said, "What have you to offer, Richard?"

"Nothing, I'm afraid. I'm sorry I can't contribute as

much as the others, but I haven't really given the question all that much thought. My position is rather different."

"I don't think it is," said Brennan, "but so long as you are willing to learn, that's all that matters.

"That leaves you, Harvey. I'm sure you'll explain to us why incentives do motivate salesmen, although, as you know, I don't believe they motivate managers."

Strong said, "The commission or incentive element has always applied to salesmen. The reason is that they are one of the few groups of people who, as Bob mentioned earlier, are assessed by results. In addition, they are 'loners', without direct control, and unlike engineers they may not even have definite calls lined up for them to make.

"Research has shown that the average salesman only works to 60 per cent of his capacity – I'm referring to work, not skills – often through lack of time-planning. The average salesman, therefore, needs incentives to drive him to try harder.

"The reasons are obvious. The salesman doesn't sign in or check out. He can start at eight o'clock in the morning, or make his first call at ten or even later. He can take his children to school every morning, or return home early every evening to take his wife shopping – and many do just that. But it is the commission element that motivates him not to waste his time. Most salesmen are usually not paid a salary that is quite high enough for their needs, and that is irrespective of how high the salary is. It is the incentive of commission that motivates them to become better time-planners.

"Don't be too hard on salesmen. How many workers would achieve a work percentage of over 60 per cent if they had no supervision whatsoever? So far as salesmen are concerned, all the standard motivators apply – encouragement, competitiveness, involvement, pride.

But most of all it is the incentive of commission that makes them pull out that little bit extra.

"I think I'm right in saying that none of us could work much harder, athough we could possibly improve our time management; but all salesmen have the opportunity of increasing sales by the simple expedient of making more calls. Most of them do make the effort, if the reward is commensurate with the effort made.

"And that is my contribution."

Coffee arrived at that moment, and there was a short break. Brennan left the room and made his way quickly to the cashier's office, where he asked if all the accounts were ready for payment.

"Yes," came the reply. "You wanted all the signed chits, didn't you?"

"Yes. But one question: If a radio telephone call were made would there be a chit signed for that?"

"No, there wouldn't. Do you want details of all calls made?"

"Yes please; also the numbers called."

"That will take a little time, Mr Brennan."

"I won't wait. I'll be back about twelve."

"I'll have everything ready for you by then."

"Thank you."

Brennan walked slowly back to the meeting room. The coffee cups had been cleared, and he began the final session.

"If responsibility means so much as a motivating force, our objective of better quality all round is assured. You have all been given responsibility for our future this week, and certainly under 'quality' conditions.

"We face a strong challenge: *How to motivate our work force so that they will forget the past and willingly carry out our plans for the future.*

"I am only going to touch on a few main points. The first is that you must no longer believe that a substantial salary rise and bonuses, or profit-sharing, motivates managers.

"At management level we all believe that bonuses and profit-sharing are incentives. How can this be? Does it mean that a manager only works half-heartedly because he doesn't receive bonuses, and will only give of his best if one is offered? If so, in my opinion, such managers are not worth retaining.

"Bonuses, etc. should be given, because extra earnings are always welcome. But they are not motivators.

"I can't believe that you, Laurie, or you, Harvey, would work more effectively if bonuses were offered."

"I agree," said Wallace. "But just the same, it's very nice to receive one."

With a smile Brennan said, "You've made the very point I was about to make myself. So long as you always remember that, although incentives are *not* motivators, lack of them can be de-motivators. By this I mean too much time can be spent by managers arguing the point that those who help in the success of a company should share in that success. And so they should! That is my present policy. We'll discuss this subject in more detail next Monday, when I shall also be giving details of your new salary scales. I think they'll please you."

Brennan paused to let the implications of his remarks sink in, then continued, "Earlier, we talked of human relations as a motivator.

"Human relations cut very little ice if the pay is poor. But if the rewards are right, then human relations can be most powerful motivators. One word of praise can work wonders.

"Mike said that there were many short-term motivators, with which I agree, and many de-motivators, with which I also agree, but few long-term motivators. Mike stressed that fairness, integrity, and honesty are long-term motivators, because they win respect.

"Another long-term motivator is leading by example,

and this applies not only in the works but throughout the organisation. I shan't insult your intelligence by listing management faults, but you can think of some of the managers you have worked with in the past, who have not set a good example – those who are too familiar, always wanting to be 'one of the boys'; those who are too tough, wishing to show how strong they are; the bad timekeepers; the long lunchers; the vacillators . . ." Brennan laughed. "What am I doing?" he said. "The very thing I said I didn't want to do, listing management faults.

"Our objective must be to set such an example to our employees that every one of them will, at some time or another, say, 'He has his faults, but I'd hate to let him down'.

"Now I want to list some of the actions that I believe motivate people:

"First, pay rises should be based on performance against set objectives.

"Secondly, there must be a strong emphasis on training, applying to everyone from apprentices to directors. Forget that some of those we train and invest in will leave us. I believe, however, that if our policy is to promote from within, we shall build such a solid foundation that the vast majority of our employees will *want* to stay with us and benefit from our prosperity.

"Most people are eager to improve their skills, and this applies particularly to technological skills, which, if learned by our employees, will not inhibit us from installing advanced machinery, or changing designs, because of the possibilities of redundancies of loyal staff.

"We shall train such employees in the new technical skills required.

"Finally, we must have regular management meetings, with the sole purpose of discovering the true feelings of our employees. We must find possible reasons for discontent before there has to be a showdown.

"I believe that if employees are treated with respect, they will enjoy their work, and when they do so, there is greater goodwill, greater productivity, and greater profitability.

"That's all!"

When the applause subsided, Laurie made a prepared thank-you speech, which was seconded by Clayton. He thanked Brennan on behalf of the wives for giving them the experience of travelling on the world's greatest liner, the QE2. For some unaccountable reason they all then shook hands before leaving the meeting room for the last time, talking animatedly. The time was eleven-fifty am.

Brennan hurried down to the cashier's office once more, and, collecting the accounts and signed chits, ran up the stairs rather than wait for one of the lifts.

In his cabin he began checking. When Vivienne entered the room he had just found what he had been seeking.

With a passing kiss that nearly missed Vivienne's cheek Brennan left the cabin and was soon in the library, where he found the London telephone directory for A–K.

Quickly he flipped through the pages, stopping at Canada Copiers. Their number did not check with the numbers on the chits.

Brennan turned over a few pages of the directory and pinpointed M. Cornell, Pont Street. That number checked with both calls from the ship.

He had found the mole.

23   The verdict

Vivienne said, "You have that faraway look which means you're not listening to a word I've been saying."

Brennan, who had been toying with a piece of toast, said, "I keep changing my mind."

"Why?"

"Because I'm still not certain if anyone else is involved."

"But isn't it better to get it over and done with as soon as possible? Why wait for a meeting at eleven o'clock? It's more like you to corner the beast – how I hate him! – tell him some home truths and throw him out before the others arrive."

"I can't do that!"

"Why not?"

"Because then the others will get his side of the story. He'll explain how he told me a few home truths, that I was leading everyone up the garden path. He'd make me look like the loser. No, everyone must hear the facts from me first, not second-hand. And I shall ask each member of the team in turn, 'Do you want to stay or go?' And I'll make it clear that I don't give a damn either way. I'm not worried."

"But you are!"

"Viv, please –"

"Sorry, darling." She leaned across the table and kissed him. "You know best."

"That's right, I do!"

Brennan stood up, stretched himself, smiled, and said, "I've always enjoyed a challenge. This changes nothing."

At ten-fifty-five am all the managers were sitting round the boardroom table at the Linklater London headquarters. Brennan entered the room at eleven am, sat down and said quickly, "First, there has to be some straight talking."

Before he could continue, Richard Hemmings interrupted with, "Bob, I insist on saying a few words first."

"No."

"But I must."

Brennan thought quickly, and decided to change his plans and let Hemmings have his say.

Hemmings began, "I can't talk for my associates, but I would have thought that before you joined us, and even afterwards, they had all given considerable thought to their futures, being unsure of the future of Linklaters. I was in only a slightly different position because of my relationship with Scott & Ballinger. If things didn't work out, Scott & Ballinger wouldn't have kept me, and nobody would jump at a financial director who had taken part in the second failure of the company."

He paused, and Brennan said quietly, "Go on."

"Some weeks ago I was approached by a head hunter on behalf of Mark Cornell. To cut a long story short, Cornell's proposition was this. He was going to return to Canada to take over as chief executive for the whole group. He wanted me to replace him as managing director for the European operation. A very good opportunity, you must admit. A challenge, and the reward was to be very high indeed. We met three times. I can't say I liked him, but he is a most persuasive person and obviously highly efficient. He entertained my wife and me at the Connaught, and later at his flat in Pont Street.

"Quite frankly, I was in a dilemma. I didn't know you too well, Bob, and I wasn't sure of your ability to win through. There are always a lot of 'ifs' and 'buts' in a case like this. However, two things made up my mind for me. One was that Cornell also tried to persuade me to get Harvey Strong to go over to his company with me."

"The bastard!" shouted Strong.

"Not really," said Hemmings. "Just a typical tycoon who only thinks of himself and his company. He wanted Harvey because he was not too happy with his own sales director. Harvey had taken business from them and, of course, Harvey's defection would have had a tremendous effect on Linklaters.

"Maybe it was my accountancy training – I don't want to claim that I'm a man of high moral principles – but I didn't like that at all. Cornell gave me a week to make up my mind. The week expired on the day we had our London meeting, where you told us all your plans for the future and your seminar on the QE2. I telephoned Cornell that evening after the meeting and told him that I couldn't make a decision that day, but I would let him know within a week. He agreed.

"You may think it was deceitful of me to join you under these conditions, but quite frankly, even at that stage I was 90 per cent certain that I was not going to join Cornell. Again, it was only my accountancy background which made me have that 10 per cent reservation.

"You may well ask, Bob, why I didn't discuss the matter with you. I didn't, because I have learned from long experience that when a managing director is told about such an offer, he believes it is a ploy to get him to match it or improve it.

"After the first full day on the ship I made up my mind. I telephoned Cornell but he wasn't at home. His wife said he was away for a couple of days.

"After you told us about Donald Powell's conversation with your secretary, I telephoned Cornell again. This time he was there, and I told him I wouldn't be joining his company. You had already convinced me, Bob, that my future was with Linklaters.

"That's about all. I wanted to make clear to you and all my colleagues, exactly what had happened."

Brennan hoped his feelings of relief didn't show. He even avoided taking a deep breath. He was glad he had made the right decision and allowed Hemmings to speak first. He decided to say nothing about his check on the telephone calls.

He heard Hemmings say, "By the way, Bob, I shall, of course, pay for the telephone calls."

Brennan smiled and said, "You needn't bother about that, Richard, though I respect your honesty. I'm very glad you're staying with us. The same applies to you, Harvey."

"I wouldn't have joined them," said Strong, "if they'd offered me a Rolls-Royce, a yacht, and a flat in Florida!"

Brennan laughed out loud. "For that," he said, "I'd have gone over to them!" The tension eased, as everyone joined in the laughter.

Hemmings said, "Before we continue with our discussions – perhaps we ought to adjourn them for a little while – I have something here to which we have all subscribed."

He pulled up a case from under the table and took out of it three bottles of Krug champagne. "It's our turn now to be the hosts," he said, "to repay you in a very small way for your hospitality."

Corks popped. Glasses were filled and handed round. The toast was, "To Bob Brennan and Linklaters!"